John K.V. Eunson was born in Shetland and moved to the mainland to see where all that North Sea Oil went to. Graduating from Edinburgh University, where he excelled at Earth Science 1, John has worked for many years in bookselling and publishing. His first book *Sheep for Beginners* was published in 2005, followed by the bestselling *Crabbit Old Buggers* in 2006. Having lived in Scotland for most of his life and being fairly interested in old things John is ideally qualified to write a book on Scottish history.

John K.V. Eunson is 42, but looks up to 18 months younger.

Also by John K. V. Eunson

The Complete Book of Mince
(*writing as René La Sagne*)

Crabbit Old Buggers

Sheep for Beginners

Caledonication

A History of Scotland. With Jokes.

JOHN K.V. EUNSON

To Verena and Ella

First published in 2008 by
HACHETTE SCOTLAND, an imprint of
HACHETTE UK

First published in paperback in 2009 by
HACHETTE SCOTLAND

1

Cataloguing in Publication Data is available from the British Library

ISBN 978 0 7553 1858 2

Designed by Viv Mullet
Typeset by Ellipsis Books Limited, Glasgow
Printed and bound in Great Britain by Clays Ltd, St Ives plc

Hachette UK's policy is to use papers that are natural, renewable
and recyclable products and made from wood grown in sustainable forests.
The logging and manufacturing processes are expected to conform
to the environmental regulations of the country of origin.

HACHETTE SCOTLAND
An Hachette UK Company
338 Euston Road
London NW1 3BH

www.hachettescotland.co.uk
www.hachette.co.uk

Contents

CONTENTS

Acknowledgements

I would first of all like to thank John Prebble, T. C. Smout, Christopher Tabraham, Ludovic Kennedy, David Ross, my Great-aunt Agnes and the numerous other wonderful Scottish historians whom I have read over the years. I would also like to thank Bob McDevitt and Wendy McCance of Hachette Books Scotland and Rona Johnson for their patience and for giving me the opportunity to write this book, as well as Beryl, Andy and Janet Abernethy, Patrick Johnson, Alison and Cathy Grieve, Margaret McShane and the many friends and colleagues who have given their time, support, knowledge and information. Finally, I would like to thank Margaret Sharp, because I forgot to mention her in the acknowledgements for my last book and Martin Thomson for helping me decorate my kitchen.

Introduction

On 16 May 2007, the leader of the Scottish National Party became First Minister of Scotland. Alex Salmond was to be at the head of a minority SNP government that had come to power after the closest fought and most controversial elections in Scotland's history, with the winning margin coming down to the MacRury family from Barra deciding not to go on holiday to Lanzarote that week, therefore allowing them to cast the decisive votes. The Labour Party who had been the dominant political party in Scotland for fifty years were shell-shocked at having lost power by such a narrow margin, but could do nothing to prevent this transfer of power other than making sure that they took their ball with them.

Therefore, 300 years after the Act of Union of 1707 – when the Scottish parliament, and by extension the nation state of Scotland voluntarily gave up its right to exist – Scotland found itself once more being run (if only within the devolved remit of the Holyrood parliament) by a party who supported an independent Scottish nation. With this, the auld lang story of the history of Scotland – which for some had ended in 1746 at the Battle of Culloden and for others had ended in 1978 when the Bay City Rollers split up – had taken a new and unpredictable turn.

The history of Scotland is dramatic, exciting, fascinating, bloody, at times tragic and consistently wet and windy. It is a story of the Celts, Picts, Britons, Irish, Scandinavians, English, Angles, Saxons, Normans, Italians, Asians, Chinese and Poles who have come to this land in the northern part of a small island on the edge of a small continent and made it into a nation that the Romans wanted nothing to do with.

It is a story of famous historical figures such as Macbeth, William Wallace, Mary, Queen of Scots and Tony Blair. It is a story of famous historical events such as Bannockburn, the Reformation, Culloden and

Argentina '78. It is a story of famous national symbols such as tartan, bagpipes, the Loch Ness Monster and Irn-Bru. And it is a story of famous national landmarks such as Edinburgh Castle, Glencoe, the Forth Bridge and the Falkirk Wheel that are known either throughout the world or at least throughout Falkirk.

The history of Scotland is also the story of the people of Scotland. The scientists, inventors, engineers, doctors and academics who gave the world the steam engine, the telephone, television, penicillin, Dolly the Sheep and reaching warp factor 8 in *Star Trek*. The poets, the novelists, the singers, the actors and the entertainers who gave the world *Auld Lang Syne*, *Peter Pan*, *Treasure Island*, *Trainspotting* and *Donald Where's Your Troosers*. And of the millions of Scots who over the centuries have left their homeland to seek opportunities and better weather around the world, taking their names, traditions, education, culture and values with them. This long and proud tradition of the Scot abroad has culminated in the 21st century with Scotland being represented by Tartan Day in the US and Canada and by Groundskeeper Willie from *The Simpsons*.

So, join me on this journey from the Battle of Mons Graupius of AD84 to the UEFA Battle of the 2008 Cup Final. Through the highs, lows and occasional bloody awfuls of the past 2,000 years of the great achievements and bitter setbacks of a nation that has been written off many, many times, but always comes back for more.

For some, Scotland is the Best Small Country In The World, while for others it is somewhere in England. But *Caledonication* is the history of a proud nation and the proud people of a country called Caledonia, then Alba and then finally Scotland. And the history of a country which, uniquely, decided that rather than running its own affairs it would set out to take over the rest of the world instead.

The Early
Slightly Vague Years

THE FIRST SCOTS

The first humans came to Scotland around 9000BC at the end of the last Ice Age, but found the midges so unbearable that they didn't come back for another 2,000 years. The first settlers in Scotland, who had this time remembered to take plenty of Skin So Soft with them, arrived around 7000BC.

The first Scots were hunters, farmers and fishermen who worked the land and the sea. They came from Europe, across the North Sea and travelled up through Britain to hunt for plentiful pigs, birds, deer and fish as well as looking forward to the future prospect of free prescription charges. They cut down trees, planted crops of oats and barley, reared cows and sheep and spent much time discussing the weather – and what with Stone Age forecasting proving to be quite unreliable, so beginning a long historic tradition that many, many years later the Scottish weatherman Ian McCaskill was happy to continue.

The Bronze Age came to Scotland around 2000BC and, although not as good as the Gold Age or Silver Age, it was still perfectly respectable. The Bronze Age enabled people to make both weapons and tankards and modern Scottish culture began.

ORKNEY AND SHETLAND

It was in the particularly ferocious gale of 1850 that an Orcadian searching for a missing washing line discovered a long-lost Stone Age village that had been hidden by sand dunes for thousands of years until uncovered by the wind. The village of Skara Brae with its well-preserved houses – including beds and furniture – is the oldest surviving human settlement in Britain; dating back to 31000BC it is even older than Stonehenge and is thought to be the birthplace of Sir Menzies Campbell.

Orkney is in fact a treasure-trove for archaeologists

with burial tombs such as Maeshowe and the standing stones that comprise the Ring of Brodgar among the numerous representations of the Stone, Bronze and Iron Ages to have been found so far. Further north, Shetland boasts the settlement of Jarlshof which, uniquely, shows evidence of constant occupation from the Stone Age through the Vikings to the Middle Ages, and even more uniquely was given the name by Sir Walter Scott who visited the site in 1814 and called it Jarlshof in his novel *The Pirate* that was set in Shetland.

From all the archaeological evidence unearthed in the Northern Isles it appears clear that a sophisticated and important society existed from ancient times, with strong trading links to the rest of Britain and a great wisdom gained from the consumption of so much fudge.

Shetland is also the home of the Shetland pony that has been bred on the islands from Bronze Age times. The Shetland breed is famous for its intelligence, sturdiness, long hair, thick coat, widely spaced eyes, stocky body, wide girth and small stature – no more than three-and-a-half feet tall – and, interestingly, the Shetland pony shares all of these characteristics.

In the Outer Hebrides on the Isle of Lewis we find the standing stones at Calanais (or Callanish). There are about fifty surviving stones that form a circle, avenues and rows and they are believed to be more than 4,000 years old. Calanais was rediscovered in the 19th century after being completely covered in peat. There is the possibility that there are more ancient wonders to discover at the Calanais site but as almost all the locals now have central heating and no longer cut peat we will probably never know.

THE CELTS

The tribes of people that we call the Celts came from central Europe and had for centuries been emigrating in a westerly direction, finally reaching Scotland around 1200BC. No one knows how inter-related the different Celtic tribes were to each other or whether they came to conquer, to settle or to look for plumbing jobs, but whatever the reasons there remain strong connections of language and culture that link the Celtic people of Scotland, Ireland, Cornwall, the Isle of Man and Brittany. It is unclear what in particular attracted the Celts to settle in such a cold, wet, mountainous country as Scotland, but perhaps like Humphrey Bogart in *Casablanca* they were simply misinformed. Or to be more accurate, once the weary Celts had finally arrived in Scotland there was nowhere else to go.

The Celtic religious leaders and wise men were called Druids, who led their people in worshipping and offering sacrifices to the gods of nature. Eventually the Druids all emigrated to Wales to appear as extras in *Doctor Who*. The Celts fished around the Scottish coast in small boats called curachs or, in Wales, coracles.

The Celts lived in stone or wooden dwellings, depending on what materials were available, the most common of which were roundhouses and they also built hill-forts which were called duns and loch shelters built on wooden poles that were called crannogs. The most famous of the Celtic buildings were the stone towers that they built from around 200BC and were called brochs. The largest surviving broch is to be found at the forty-foot (13m) high Mousa Broch on the island of Mousa in Shetland. These brochs did not have any windows as the Celts realised what they lost in enjoying the view they gained in what they saved on double glazing costs.

The Iron Age succeeded the Bronze Age by 400BC and transformed Scotland through the production of iron tools and weapons, such as harnesses for horses, chariots, helmets and swords, and would change Scotland forever through the invention of Irn-Bru.

THE ROMANS

The all-conquering Italians came to Scotland in AD79 and called it Caledonia. The Romans had invaded Britain in AD43 as part of their world tour but had concentrated on defeating the tribes of England and establishing their rule before heading north. The Romans defeated the Caledonians at the Battle of Mons Graupius, probably somewhere in Aberdeenshire, in AD83. The reason that we know of this battle is that the Romans brought the written word to Scotland and were keen to leave for posterity a record of how great they were. The Roman leader was called Agricola and his nephew was the historian Tacitus. It was Tacitus who wrote of the battle of Mons Graupius and the Caledonian leader Calgacus, the first Scot to make the annals of history, who was attributed with the quote about Scotland, 'We are the last people on earth and the last of the free', and the quote about the Romans, 'They make a desert and call it peace' – presumably in response to the invaders' policy of burning local villages rather than a comment about the Italians pudding-making skills.

Tacitus wrote that the battle of Mons Graupius saw a force of 30,000 Caledonians defeated by an army of 20,000 Romans, although when his report was edited Mons Graupius became Mons Grampius by mistake, which in turn was translated into the Grampian Mountains.

It was Tacitus who also wrote of Agricola sailing up the east coast and around the top of the Scottish mainland where the Romans believed they saw Thule, the legendary land of the North beyond all known boundaries. Thule today is a pub on the Lerwick harbour-front in Shetland, complete with pool table.

HADRIAN'S WALL

The Romans did not seem to be too enamoured of the Northern outpost of their Empire, the only philosophical reason for them coming to Scotland seemed to be because it was there. They built a series of forts between the Forth and the Clyde, reaching as far north as what is now Perth, and then in the 2nd century began the building of two massive walls that crossed the entire country – Hadrian's Wall in the south and the 35-mile long, 10-feet high Antonine Wall in the north. The Antonine Wall spanned Scotland from the Firth of Forth in the east to the Firth of Clyde in the west and was completed in AD142, a not too subtle way of marking what the Romans perceived was the end of civilisation as they knew it.

The Romans did not stay long in Scotland. They were never able to fully suppress the Caledonian tribes that they encountered and their presence consisted of large military garrisons that were expensive to maintain. Around AD120 the famous Ninth Legion was sent north to fight the Caledonian tribes and was never seen again, presumably implying that the legionnaires were massacred rather than that they settled and opened a string of pizzerias.

Faced with constant attacks, by AD160 the Romans had abandoned the Antonine Wall and retreated behind Hadrian's Wall thus leaving Caledonia for good, although they remained in Britain until AD410. The locals celebrated, as was their wont, with 300 years of raiding across the Wall, sporadic tribal battles and carving birds on big stones.

A legend has built up that Pontius Pilate was actually born in Fortingall in Perthshire. There appears to be no evidence whatsoever to back up this claim that Pilate was Scottish, but as there is little information about where his actual birthplace was, as far as the rest of Europe is concerned, if we want him then we can have him.

MIDGES

One of the reasons why the Romans did not settle in Scotland and did not go further north than Perthshire and the Antonine Wall must surely have been because of the Highland midge. The midge is found throughout the world, but the Highland midge, especially on the West Coast, is one of the most ferocious – midges are partial to wet land that has not been cultivated and mild weather.

It is the female midge who bites, as she can only lay her eggs after tasting blood. They do not like wind or bright sunlight, prefer dark to light clothing and are most active in mornings and evenings. The midge lives for around twenty-five days and they are at their peak during July and August. Worryingly, if one midge bites you then this sets off a chemical reaction that attracts several thousand more. Midges do not just attack humans but will bite any mammal, however sheep and deer tend to be more phlegmatic about the problem and are less likely to go indoors or order expensive anti-midge machines. As any Cheviot will tell you, if there are likely to be up to ten million midges per acre, what is the use of a bloody machine?

THE PICTS

The name Picts comes from the Latin *Picti* meaning painted ones and was first recorded by the Romans in AD297. They were awarded their reputation as a ferocious people by the Romans whose garrisons they attacked frequently and who at no time were able to subdue them and who were, therefore, not especially fond of them. Although some believe that the Picts might have predated the Celts, it is now thought that they were of Celtic origin and became the dominant people in Scotland from Fife in the south to Shetland in the north. The Picts remained in Scotland long after the Romans had gone, with Pictish kings of a united Pictland being recorded from around AD600 onwards.

The Picts became famous for carving intricate designs on standing stones and, with their use of woad, inventing the popular children's pastime of face-painting. In Aberlemno in Angus you will find four large Pictish stones and slabs with designs of a cross, animals and a scene thought to depict the Battle of Nechtansmere in AD685 when the Picts defeated the Northumbrians. The Northumbrians are shown wearing helmets with long nose guards, the Picts are bare headed; it is not known whether this is an accurate depiction of the headwear of the time or whether the sculptor just grew tired of having to carve helmets.

COLUMBA

If the Roman Empire had decided to leave Scotland well alone, the Church of Rome was to prove more persistent. Saint Ninian (AD360–432) was either the first missionary to bring Christianity to Scotland or the first missionary to live to tell the tale. He established a church at Whithorn in Galloway.

Saint Kentigern was a 6th-century missionary in Strathclyde and established the first church in Glasgow on the site where Glasgow Cathedral was built, rebuilt and where it continues to stand today. Saint Kentigern is also know as Saint Mungo as he thought it was an easier name for people to remember than Kentigern and he wasn't keen on being called Mary or Midge.

Other missionaries followed over the centuries, most bearing the same first name – Saint. The most famous was Columba (521–97), an Irish monk who founded a monastery on the island of Iona, which would become a major centre for Christianity and learning.

Columba, which translates from old Irish (Colum-cille) as 'Dove of the Church', was born in

Donegal and was of Irish royal descent. He was exiled from Ireland in 563 after causing an Irish family dispute which turned nasty, thereafter he devoted his life's work to making amends by converting as many heathen Scots as possible. He left Ireland with twelve followers, although there was considerable disagreement about which one was going to take on the Judas role, and finally settled on Iona from where – as part of the agreement of his exile – he was unable to see the coast of Ireland from any part of the island, or phone home at weekends.

Columba is accredited with many miracles and the conversion of Brude, the king of the Picts. Columba had travelled all the way to Inverness to see the heathen king only to find that he was barred entry to Brude's fortress. At this point Columba loudly prayed to God for the gates to open and made the sign of the Cross, at which point the gates were flung open and the milkman came out after completing his round.

The 8th-century casket, the Monymusk Reliquary that currently resides in the Museum of Scotland, is believed to have also once contained some small bones of Saint Columba's. Legend has it that at the Battle of Bannockburn in 1314, the Monymusk Reliquary was the 'Brecbennoch' carried proudly into battle by the Scottish army, successfully distracting the English who spent the next few hours wondering what could be in the box.

IONA

On his death on 9 June 597, Columba prophesied that Scottish kings and people from many nations would gravitate to Iona for centuries to come – although whether he had in mind the Viking raiders who would turn up 200 years later is debatable.

The beautifully illuminated *Book of Kells*, which contains the four gospels of the New Testament is believed to have been partly or wholly written on Iona sometime around AD800. The manuscript was taken to Ireland for safekeeping and is now on display at Trinity College Dublin.

Iona long remained an important place for the early Scottish kings; they would make pilgrimages to the sacred isle and many chose to be buried there – even after Columba's relics had been removed from the island and taken to Dunkeld in the 9th century.

Iona was a very important Christian centre and Christianity was to become the dominant religion in Scotland by the 9th century. As the Christians were the only ones who could write, we have only the

Christians' word on how seamless and peaceful this conversion was – and they, after all, were on a mission from God.

CELTIC CROSS

By the 9th century the Celtic Church became the dominant form of Christianity in Scotland and took as its symbol the Celtic cross – although pre-Christian in origin, it was accepted as the cross of Christ surrounded by a ring said to represent the sun, so combining Christianity with traditional pagan beliefs. The most famous example in Scotland is the 9th-century St Martin's Cross which stands outside Iona Abbey. The Celtic cross is one of the best-known and most prevalent motifs in Celtic art and it is used frequently on jewellery, stationery, stencils and transfers. Celtic crosses have also become a common tattoo design and have been known to pop up sometimes when least expected.

LOCH NESS MONSTER

Saint Columba was also famous for having seen the Loch Ness Monster in 565, one of the earliest recorded reports of Nessie. Apparently, however, it was later explained to Columba that what he thought was a monster was actually an overweight otter, but embarrassed by his mistake he kept this information to himself.

Throughout the centuries the monster has been 'seen' from time to time but Nessie became internationally famous in 1933 when several sightings of a large creature in the loch were reported to the press. In 1934, the famous photograph of 'Nessie' taken on 1 April by surgeon Robert Wilson was published and, for decades, people flocked to the loch with renewed hope of glimpsing the creature. Doubts began to circulate about the veracity of the surgeon's photograph with some experts stating that on close inspection the monster in the picture could not be more than three feet long and, in 1994, the surgeon's son finally revealed that his father's picture had been taken as a practical joke.

Over the years, several scientific studies have been carried out on Loch Ness in an effort to establish incontrovertible evidence of the creature's existence but, so far, without success. Despite this, and the reduction of sightings in recent years, it is still believed by some scientists and many involved in that region's tourist industry that Nessie is a plesiosaur whose family survived the species' general extinction sixty-five million years ago and moved to Loch Ness when it was created by the last Ice Age 10,000 years ago, although they admit that it's still unclear at what stage the monster began to wear a tartan bonnet.

STRATHCLYDE

In the south west of Scotland was the Kingdom of Strathclyde (which also included parts of Cumbria) and its capital was at Dumbarton Rock. Strathclyde was the last bastion of a Celtic Britain which had been defeated in England by the Angles and Saxons and its people spoke a language similar to Welsh – the names of places such as Lanark, Paisley and Glasgow come from this heritage. Glasgow means 'green hollow' although a large percentage of Glaswegians remain convinced that the hollow was actually blue.

Dumbarton was captured by the Vikings in 871 but remained the capital of an independent Strathclyde until the 11th century. Dumbarton became famous many centuries later as the birthplace – in 1952 – of David Byrne, lead singer of Talking Heads. The Byrne family moved to America when David was only two years old, although it has been said that his most famous hit *Road To Nowhere* was influenced by his birthplace.

THE SCOTS

By the 8th century AD, what we now call Scotland was divided into four distinct regions. The Scots began arriving from Ireland in the 5th century. Their name came from the Latin name *Scotti* that translates as raiders or pirates, not as an annoying small dog as one might expect. The Scots, who had emigrated from Northern Ireland and were concentrated in Argyll and the west, were Gaelic speaking and called their kingdom Dalriada or Dal Riata.

The Picts were concentrated in the north of Scotland in Perthshire, Aberdeenshire and the Highlands. The Celtic Britons of the Kingdom of Strathclyde and the Angles, who with the Saxons had come to Britain from Germany and had conquered most of England, ruled in Northumbria and Lothian in the south-east of Scotland. It was the Angles who would give their name to the country of England and they spoke an early form of the English that would eventually become Scotland's national language.

KENNETH MACALPIN

In 843, Kenneth MacAlpin (800–858) who was king of Scots also became king of the Picts. The previous Pictish king had died in battle against the Vikings and Kenneth was able to gain the vacant throne by the traditional method of killing every Pictish claimant, and a few more for good luck, that he could find. For many years Picts and Scots had at times joined together to fight common enemies, and alliances by marriage were not uncommon, but it was Kenneth's dynasty that joined Pict and Scot together and became the royal line of Scotland culminating in Hamish McAlpine, the legendary Dundee United goalkeeper. The accession of Kenneth marked the beginning of the decline of the Picts as they became assimilated and submerged into a Scottish Gaelic identity, forgotten by history as a result of their failure to learn to read and write.

The new kingdom of Picts and Scots was given the Gaelic name, Alba, and King Kenneth I made Perthshire the political, religious and royal focus of this new country (Strathclyde and Lothian were still separate kingdoms). Kenneth had taken Saint Columba's relics from Iona to the monastery at Dunkeld that would later become the site of the beautiful medieval Dunkeld Cathedral. His new capital was to be found at nearby Scone with the famous Stone of Destiny as the symbol of the nation.

THE STONE OF DESTINY

The Stone of Destiny is an ancient block of sandstone of uncertain origins. Some claim it came from Ireland with the Scots when they settled in their new kingdom of Dalriada, others say that it was the Biblical stone that Jacob slept on before the days of roll pillows and came to Scotland from Egypt while others still say it had been blessed by either Saint Patrick, or Saint Columba, or both. However, from the time of Kenneth MacAlpin the Stone at Scone was where all Scottish kings were crowned and was thus literally as well as symbolically the seat of government.

Scone is also the name of a lightly sweetened Scottish cake that has become popular around the world. Scones are traditionally served with a nice pot of tea and eaten with butter or with butter and jam, although heaven help you if you ask for jam and no butter.

Is This A Country
I See Before Me

ALBA

The union of Scots and Picts did not a nation make and it was to be another 200 years before Scotland was even vaguely unified. England had become a unified Anglo-Saxon kingdom in the 10th century and Lothian and the Borders were part of that kingdom. The English Angles remained in the Lothian and Borders areas while Strathclyde, although increasingly under the influence of the Scots, retained its own kings until the 11th century. Yet a new threat was to appear in the north from over the sea in the form of the Vikings, who, like the Romans before them, had a passion for foreign travel.

THE VIKINGS

The first recorded raid by the Vikings on Scotland was in 794. The following year, the un-Christian Vikings raided the holy island of Iona for the first time, burning down Saint Columba's church in the process. It is believed that it was at this time the *Book of Kells* was saved and taken to Ireland for safekeeping. In fact, the Vikings were to raid Iona so often that even today islanders are still uneasy at the thought of Norwegian tourists.

The early period of the Vikings in Scotland was characterised by targeting Christian centres where they knew that there were substantial financial rewards. Not surprisingly, the Christian chroniclers of the time did not record the Scandinavians in a favourable light. However, the Vikings appear to have become tired of incessant raping and pillaging and began to settle in the north and south-west of mainland Scotland and in the Western and Northern Isles. They brought their language, customs with them and gave Viking names to the places where they settled but they converted to Christianity to help them settle in better with their neighbours.

Most of the place names in Orkney and Shetland today are of Viking or Norse origin, indeed Norse place names remain scattered throughout Scotland.

An example of this is the Norse word *wick*, meaning bay, which can be found in Wick, Lerwick and the less well known Getsonmywick.

Over the ensuing centuries the Vikings continued to settle in Scotland, building ships, writing long poems and making helmets with horns stuck on briefly fashionable. Some of the history of this time is recorded in the 13th century *Orkneyinga Saga* that tells the story of such characters as Thorfinn the Mighty, Sigurd the Stout, Magnus Barelegs and the slimmer, and more soberly dressed Earl Magnus the Martyr (Orkney's Saint Magnus).

Earl Magnus became joint ruler with his cousin Earl Haakon in 1105. Magnus was known for being devout and seeking peace, but around 1117 he was betrayed and captured by Haakon. Haakon had sworn an oath not to kill an unarmed man and Magnus, fearing for his cousin's immortal soul, suggested to Haakon that, instead of killing him, he (Magnus) was happy to leave Orkney forever on a pilgrimage, or to be exiled and imprisoned on the Scottish mainland, or that Haakon might 'have me mutilated in anyway you choose . . .'. Haakon, however, decided to ignore these options and had Magnus killed by his cook who, presumably, was having a day off from working in the kitchen. In honour of the saintly Magnus, work began in 1137 in

Kirkwall on St Magnus Cathedral. The cathedral was – and remains – the most northerly in Britain and in 1997 was the venue for the last ever show of the original *Mastermind* TV series hosted by the saint's namesake Magnus Magnusson.

After centuries of vilification the reputation of the Vikings has been rehabilitated and festivals such as the Shetland's Up Helly Aa festival, held every January celebrate the island's Norse heritage and the ability of Shetlanders to drink steadily through until six in the morning while maintaining possession of a large axe.

LOTHIAN

Over the next hundred years, the kingdom of Alba had to endure repeated Viking attacks and numerous crushing defeats but were saved ultimately by the Scandinavians' lack of unity and – again, in common with the Romans – the distinct impression that, compared to England, Ireland, France or even America, Scotland was not really worth the bother.

The new kingdom of England however was much more interested in Alba and King Athelstan defeated King Constantine II of Scotland in 934 and became the first monarch to state English sovereignty of

Scotland and the first to demand that Scotland pledge allegiance. A further battle took place in 937 in which Athelstan defeated Constantine's combined invading force which included the armies of King Owen of Strathclyde and the Irish Viking king of Dublin. The battle took place at Brunanburh (or Brunanburgh), the site of which may have been as far south as The Wirral in north-west England or further north in what is now south-west Scotland. Athelstan's victory at Brunanburh confirmed England as the major power in the British Isles, or so we are told by the English historians of the time.

In 973 Lothian (then part of the kingdom of Northumbria) was given to King Kenneth II of Alba by the Anglo-Saxon king, Edgar, in return for a pledge of loyalty and being willing to row, along with the other non-Anglo-Saxon kings of Britain, Edgar's royal barge at Chester. There was a scary moment when Kenneth II's dodgy back looked like it might flare up, but a quick massage and two painkillers later and Kenneth was able to row and Lothian became considered part of Scotland.

Even then, it was not until 1018 when Alba's King Malcolm II defeated the English army at Carham on the River Tweed that the land to the south of the Forth estuary – including Edinburgh and Lothian – was finally, and decisively, won by Scotland and the Tweed became the kingdom's southern boundary. And it was not until 1034 – when the last king of Strathclyde, Owen the Bald, gave up his throne when a hair transplant went badly wrong – that Strathclyde, too, was absorbed by Malcolm II and the nation we recognise today as Scotland came in to being. A nation that was Celtic, Christian and, mostly Gaelic-speaking, but more likely to use the new anglicised name 'Scotland' rather than its original name 'Alba' in an early example of political rebranding.

MONARCHY

Between the union of the kingdoms of Picts and Scots by Kenneth MacAlpin in AD843 and the Union of the Crowns under James VI of Scotland in 1603 there were forty-three Scottish monarchs in total – although there is a little vagueness at times during the 9th century about who exactly was king.

The king's name scoring the highest Roman numeral count by 1603 is James, with a total of six. James has remained a very popular first name in Scotland to this day although one of its derivations, Jamie, is now as common a given name as James. Other derivations include Jim, Jimmy, Jamesie and Jeemsie. Famous Scottish James's include inventor of the steam engine James Watt and *Peter Pan* author James M. Barrie.

Almost as popular is Malcolm – there were four kings of that name and derivations include Malky. The name Malcolm means follower of Saint Columba and famous Malcolms include Conservative MP Sir Malcolm Rifkind and black power leader Malcolm X, who was anything but conservative.

Four names appear three times in the Scottish kings' roll call: Robert, Alexander, Kenneth and Constantine. The first King Robert was better known as Robert the Bruce while other famous Scottish Roberts include author Robert Louis Stevenson and national bard Robert Burns. Roberts may also be referred to as Rob, Robbie, Bert, Bertie, Bob, Bobby and, if you're particularly unlucky, Boaby. A shortened version of the name Alexander has been chosen by football manager Alex Ferguson and First Minister Alex Salmond and in other truncated forms it appears as Lex, Eck, Alec, Sandy and Zander. Kenneth originates from the Gaelic/Pictish Cináed/Ciniod and means born of fire. Famous Kenneths include the late Kenneth

Williams, star of the *Carry On* films and Scottish footballer Kenny Dalglish.

Unlike those Scottish monarchs' monikers that remain popular today, Constantine appears to have gone out of fashion some time in the 10th century and shows no sign of ever reappearing.

PLACE NAMES

Many of Scotland's best-known place names came into being by the 11th century. These names would have a variety of linguistic sources – Gaelic, Celtic Britonnic, Norse, English and Scots – emphasising the different peoples and kingdoms that made up the new nation.

For example, the Britonnic word for 'where waters meet' is *Aber* as in Aberdeen, Abernethy and Aberfeldy; the Gaelic word *dún* meaning hill or fort became dun as in Dundee and Dunfermline and the Lowland Scots, the Norse and Scots word for church is *kirk* as in Kirkcaldy and Falkirk.

Place names have also long been given as first names and surnames, and the names of islands – such as Skye meaning either winged or winged island from the Gaelic or misty isle from the Norse and Iona, meaning either yew tree or island – are now popular girls' names. The most popular boys' name in Scotland today is Lewis and the name of the island is believed to come from the Norse meaning homes of the people, although it can be argued that the name has also become popular through fans of *Inspector Morse*.

SAINT ANDREW

Saint Andrew was one of Jesus' twelve apostles and the younger brother of Simon Peter (Saint Peter). Legend has it that in the 4th century some of the saint's bones were rescued from his tomb in Constantinople by a Greek monk, Saint Regulus (Saint Rule), who – due to Andrew's little reported love of golf – brought the relics to what would, eventually, become the city of St Andrews in Fife.

Condemned to death by the Romans in Patras, Greece, in the 1st century but considering himself unworthy to die in the same way as Jesus, Saint Andrew was crucified on a diagonal cross. In AD832 during the battle of Athelstaneford in Lothian at which Picts and Scots fought the Angles of Northumbria, a vision of Saint Andrew appeared to the Pictish king promising him victory, despite the odds being stacked against his army. The following day, a diagonal white cross – the saltire – was seen against the blue sky and this inspired the king's men to overcome the Angles. Thus, from 1160 when the chapel which had housed the saint's relics was replaced by St Andrews Cathedral – and his relics moved there – the city promptly became Scotland's mainland religious centre; the saltire was adopted as Scotland's national flag; Saint Andrew became the country's patron saint and his feast day, 30 November, became Scotland's national day where traditionally it is celebrated by being completely ignored.

MACBETH

In 1034 Malcolm II was succeeded on the throne by his grandson Duncan I, however in 1040 Duncan was defeated and killed near Elgin in Morayshire by rebels led by the ruler of Moray who was called Macbeth. Macbeth then ruled Scotland relatively successfully for the next seventeen years – even finding time in 1050 to go with his wife (Kenneth II's granddaughter) to Rome on an extended weekend city break. In 1057 Macbeth was defeated and killed by forces led by Duncan's son Malcolm Canmore at the Battle of Lumphanan in Aberdeenshire.

Macbeth was little more than a footnote in the course of Scottish history, and would have remained just that were it not for a certain Englishman by the name of William Shakespeare who wrote a little play about him around 1604–06. It is unlikely that Macbeth would have been too pleased with Shakespeare's portrait of him, or with the playwright's mix of fact and fiction – the real-life Macbeth was never confirmed Thane of Glamis or Thane of Cawdor and he did not die at Dunsinane Castle, which is in Perthshire. And if Lady Macbeth (real name Gruoch) had ever encountered the bard who inflicted upon her that 'damn'd spot', she would undoubtedly have gone looking for him with specially sharpened knives.

Long-held superstition in theatrical circles compels actors to shun any mention of the 'M' word and refer only to 'the Scottish play' in the belief that to speak the work's title brings bad luck to the company performing the play. Shakespeare's tragedy, it is thought, is cursed. Theories about why any utterance of the 'M' word is a portent of doom vary from Shakespeare writing real witches' spells into the original text and actors being stabbed when real daggers were used mistakenly in an early production, to the excruciating pain inflicted on audiences by actors' extremely bad attempts at Scottish accents.

MALCOLM AND MARGARET

Malcolm Canmore (1031–93) was crowned Malcolm III in 1058, much preferring his new name to that of Canmore which was often translated as 'Big Head'. After his first wife, Ingibjorg, died, Malcolm married Margaret (1046–1093), an Anglo-Saxon princess who had been exiled in Scotland after the Norman Conquest of 1066. Margaret was the sister of Edgar, the main Saxon claimant to the English throne from which he was excluded by William I, and it is said that they were on their way to Europe for safety when they were shipwrecked at what became known as St Margaret's Hope near Edinburgh. Margaret found sanctuary with the widowed Malcolm who married her and, in return, his queen brought 'civilising' Saxon and Norman influences to the Scottish court: Gaelic was replaced by the English language and devout Catholicism was practised.

The reign of Malcolm and Margaret was concentrated at their new royal court at Dunfermline and Malcolm launched repeated attempts to claim land in the north of England from the Normans. These attacks were to prove ultimately unsuccessful – in 1073 he had to promise his loyalty to the English King William I (the Conqueror) and, finally, Malcolm III was killed in battle at Alnwick in 1093.

Margaret died on hearing of her husband's death and was canonised in 1249. The long-standing popularity of the name Margaret in Scotland began with Queen Margaret and so it remained until 1979 and Mrs Thatcher.

Four of Malcolm's sons reigned in succession from 1094 until 1153 – Duncan II (Malcolm's only son by Ingibjorg), then Edgar (not a name that was to catch on), Alexander I and David I.

EDINBURGH CASTLE

The oldest surviving building in Edinburgh stands within Edinburgh Castle's walls; St Margaret's Chapel was built at the beginning of the 12th century by Queen Margaret's son David I in honour of his mother. Throughout the first millennium AD there had been a fortress on Castle Rock – the location of the current castle – which gave the castle and surrounding settlement its Brythonic name *Dyn* (later *Din*) *Eidyn* meaning, possibly, fortress on a rock. The Northumbrian Angles captured the fort in the 7th century and renamed it *Edin-burgh*. The Scots did not recapture their future capital city until 954, and even then kept its English name rather than the, by then Gaelic *Dùn Èideann* which, many years later, they would kindly donate to the New Zealand city of

Dunedin – famous for its university and nearby albatross colony.

DAVID I

David I spent his youth at court in Norman England and, as a result, it was during his reign (1124–53) that Scotland saw the introduction of a feudal system with land and power given to the king's nobles and worked by peasants. In return, the nobles agreed to support the Crown and to build numerous sturdy castles and abbeys.

Many of these nobles were new, Anglo-Norman knights who further established the English language in Scotland, that evolved into Scots, that became the language of trade and administration as well as that of the Court, thus continuing the long process of English displacing Gaelic as the language of Scotland. The Normans also brought new surnames to Scotland, such as Fraser, Menzies, Graham, Murray, Bruce and Forsyth and were therefore responsible not only for naming Scotland's most famous future king but also game-show host Bruce Forsyth.

David I also continued his mother's reform of the Celtic Church, bringing it yet more in line with the Church of Rome. This included ending the Celtic Church's tradition that monks were allowed to marry, meaning that from that point on Scottish women had to look elsewhere to find attractive, well-educated bald men.

It was also in the reign of David that the first Scottish coins were produced, although they were immediately regarded with suspicion by London taxi-drivers of the time.

THE LION RAMPANT

David I had finally managed to achieve the goal of claiming Northumberland and Cumberland from England as part of Scotland in 1136, but his successor Malcolm IV soon lost them again and relations between the two countries remained fraught. When David I's grandson, William I of Scotland (r1165–1214) unsuccessfully invaded England in 1174 and managed to get himself captured at Alnwick, he was kept prisoner and released only after paying a ransom, accepting England's supremacy over Scotland and promising never to do it again.

William was able to buy back Scotland in 1189 for 10,000 silver marks (he had been given first refusal over any future transfers) as the new English king, Richard I, required money to raise an army to join the Crusades. William himself was to join a later crusade and chose as his banner a red lion rampant on a yellow background. An animal with less connection to Scotland it would be hard to find, but lions were traditionally used in heraldry as a symbol of battle and William was of the opinion that a standard with a Highland cow on it was just not that intimidating at the head of an army. The Lion Rampant was adopted as the Royal Standard of Scotland and, even though officially only the monarchy or representatives of the monarchy are allowed to fly the Standard, it has become accepted as Scotland's second national flag and also appears on the badge of the Scottish football team.

William was later to be given the soubriquet 'William the Lion' not, it appears, because of his Standard, but because he liked to stay in bed until late in the morning.

GLASGOW

By the 12th century the population of Glasgow had risen to well over 1,000 and the urban settlement was given the title of Royal Burgh in 1175. Work began in the late 12th century on the magnificent Glasgow Cathedral on the site of St Mungo's original chapel. To celebrate Glasgow's new-found fame an annual fair was declared in 1197, which led to the establishment of the Glasgow Fair Fortnight; this annual two-week holiday continues to this day, a tradition for which generations of Blackpool's bed and breakfast and guesthouse proprietors have remained eternally grateful.

THE HIGHLANDS

Despite ongoing disputes with England, Malcolm and Margaret's dynasty was firmly established in the increasingly prosperous and increasingly anglicised Lowlands of Scotland; towns grew, royal burghs were established, farms thrived and landowners grew rich – and the Royal Court, nobles and landowners spoke Lowland Scots (Anglo-Scots). However, this was not the case in the rest of the country. The Highlands remained populated by Gaelic-speaking clans who depended on subsistence farming and fishing.

A key part of their farming was Highland cattle or Hielan coos that were bred in either red or black and became famous for their shaggy coats and long horns. Highland cattle are thought to be one of the oldest cattle breeds in the world and groups of Highland cattle are called folds rather than herds because in olden times they were kept in open stone shelters called folds to protect them from bad weather.

Before he became a Beatle, the late John Lennon would as a young boy spend many happy summer holidays at Durness in Sutherland where there were many cattle and it has been suggested that the Highland cow's floppy fringe would later inspire the famous Beatles' haircut. Lennon would never forget his time in Scotland and returned in 1963 with The Beatles to play a sold-out concert at Dingwall Town Hall.

LORDS OF THE ISLES

The west coast of Scotland and Western Isles from Lewis to the Isle of Man were, by the beginning of the 13th century, still ruled by ancestors of the Celtic Vikings. They had pledged allegiance to Norway and were led by warlords such as Somerled – who declared himself 'King of Mann and the Isles' in the 12th century – and were wholly beyond the reach of the Scottish Crown.

In 1263 Alexander III defeated King Haakon IV of Norway's fleet of at the battle of Largs then in 1266 Alexander and Haakon's successor Magnus IV of Norway signed the Treaty of Perth with which sovereignty over the Western Isles and the Isle of Man was restored to Scotland. The Battle of Largs is still celebrated today with a wide range of quality ice-cream shops along the sea front.

Despite the outcome of the Battle of Largs

Alexander failed to gain any meaningful control over the Western Isles. Accepting Alexander as their overlord in name only, the MacDonalds from Islay (former vassals of the Norwegian king) retained their possession of the isles and determined to become the most powerful clan in the Hebrides. From 1336 the MacDonalds declared each successive heir-apparent Lord of the Isles and managed to avoid all attempts to usurp them until 1493 when James IV took both their title and their extensive lands. In the end, James V of Scotland granted the Lordship to the heirs-apparent to the Crown and there it remains to this day with Prince Charles (1948–) the current holder. Charles caused controversy in his role as Lord when in 1963 he was caught ordering an alcoholic drink in a Stornoway bar. This caused a huge scandal at the time, not because Charles was aged only fourteen but because of all the alcoholic drinks he could have chosen in a Hebridean bar, he chose a cherry brandy.

LEWIS CHESSMEN

The Lewis chessmen are intricately carved chess pieces that were discovered on the Isle of Lewis sometime before 1831. There are ninety-three pieces in total and it is believed that they were made in the 12th century in Norway before being transported to the Hebrides, possibly on route to be traded in Ireland. Eleven of the pieces are on display at the National Museum of Scotland in Edinburgh, the remainder are exhibited at the British Museum in London. That the collection has been divided has caused considerable controversy, with some arguing that this has contributed to the chessmen's glum expressions, although most experts believe the problem is not so much that the pieces are housed in separate locations, but that nobody has worked out whose move it is.

THE NORTHERN ISLES

The Northern Islands of Orkney and Shetland remained under Norwegian control but by the 15th century the crown of Norway had been united with the crown of Denmark. In 1469 James III of Scotland agreed to marry the daughter of the Danish king Christian I. As the proud father of the bride Christian was obliged to provide a dowry but he was suffering a little cash flow problem so, in case he should fall short the agreed sum, pawned Orkney and Shetland to the Scottish Crown. Unfortunately, after a particularly bad run on the horses, Christian could not find the necessary funds and in 1472 Orkney and Shetland were incorporated into Scotland.

Over the centuries several half-hearted attempts were made to look into repaying the debt and reclaiming the islands, and from time-to-time several Orcadians and Shetlanders wondered wistfully if life might not be better under the Danes. But the debt was never repaid and the only subsequent Viking invasion has been in recent years, when Norwegians and Faroese make landfall at Lerwick because, compared to their homelands, the price of alcohol – even in Shetland – is incredibly cheap.

SCOTTISH ISLANDS

The largest and most highly populated Scottish island is Lewis and Harris with some 20,000 inhabitants and a geographical area of 2,180 square kilometres. The main town is Stornoway and the island is home to nearly half of all Scotland's remaining Gaelic speakers. Confusingly, although Lewis and Harris is one island, they are known separately as the Isle of Lewis (to the north) and the Isle of Harris. Lewis and Harris are both popular boys' names in Scotland and are an ideal choice for twins.

The second most populated island in Scotland is Mainland, the largest of more than one hundred islands that comprise Shetland, with a population of 17,500 – the majority in and around the main town of Lerwick. The collective shape of the islands inspired the name Shetland which comes from the Norse *Hjaltland* meaning dagger land. The Scandinavian influence continued long after Shetland came under Scotland's wing in 1472; Norn, a now-extinct Norse language, was spoken until the 19th century yet Norse influences remain to this day in the distinctive Shetland dialect.

The third most populated island in Scotland is Orkney's Mainland whose population is 15,000. Here, the main town is Kirkwall and the locals' sing-song accent sounds not dissimilar to Welsh – or, alternatively, the Welsh accent sounds not dissimilar to Orcadian.

The fourth most populated island in Scotland, and second largest geographically, is the Isle of Skye, with a population of 9,000. The main town is Portree. Skye is still considered to be an island despite becoming connected to the Scottish mainland by the Skye Bridge which was opened in 1995.

Four other West Coast islands are each home to more than 2,000 people: Bute, main town

Rothesay; Arran, main town Brodick; Islay, main town Port Ellen, and home to eight whisky distilleries; Mull, main town Tobermory. It was the brightly painted shoreside village of Tobermory that inspired the BBC TV children's series *Balamory*, first screened in 2002. Another BBC TV children's series – this one first screened in 1973 – *The Wombles* featured a character called Tobermory who performed the role of handyman, or to be technically correct, handywomble.

ALEXANDER III AND THE MAID

Alexander III of Scotland (r1249–86) was only eight years old when he succeeded his father to the throne and only ten when he married the daughter of Henry III of England at York. At the wedding, the English king tried to make his young Scottish counterpart promise loyalty to him but the young Alexander stubbornly declined, as he had not been given the mobile phone he was promised.

Alexander grew up to become a strong and able leader, but unfortunately his queen and heirs died before he did, making him the last male of the immediate first generation Canmore line. To address this, in 1285 Alexander married again, this time choosing a bride much younger than himself. Then, one evening when he was racing home along the Fife coast, unsurprisingly quite keen to be with his betrothed, his horse stumbled near Kinghorn and threw Alexander over a cliff into the Firth of Forth.

The next in line to the throne was Alexander's granddaughter Margaret. The fact that she was female was a problem – but not an insurmountable problem; more worrying was that Margaret was aged only three and lived in Norway. Incidentally, as far as we know, the horse was fine.

EDWARD I

The English king, Edward I (1239–1307) – who had already subjugated the Welsh – saw the death of Alexander III as an opportunity to reassert English supremacy over Scotland and proposed a marriage – which would unite the two kingdoms – between his son and heir, Edward, and, when she came of age, the Scottish queen. Realising that this was actually more of an 'offer that they could not refuse', the Scottish nobles agreed to Edward's proposal – but in the hope that they could come up with an alternative before Margaret reached marriageable age.

Sadly for Margaret (who was given the suffix Maid

of Norway), she was never to marry Prince Edward, or anybody else for that matter. The voyage that should have brought her from Norway to Scotland in 1290 ran into a storm which blew the ship off course and made seven-year-old Margaret ill. The ship made landfall in Orkney – then, under Norwegian sovereignty – and there, never having set foot on Scottish soil – Margaret died. It has been mooted that the young queen died as a result of terrible seasickness, although Margaret's cook did say that he wasn't so sure about the fish.

Margaret's death brought to an end the rule of House of Canmore. The Scottish Royal line which had begun with Malcolm III was no more, leading to the appearance of no fewer than thirteen hopefuls all claiming some kind of distant connection to the House of Canmore. The Scots themselves had no idea which of thirteen should be their king so they turned to England and Edward I to make the decision for them.

Edward agreed to adjudicate, and in 1292 came to Berwick Castle to interview all the claimants in a very early Royal edition of *The X Factor*, with the lucky winner also having to agree to swear allegiance – in this case to King Edward rather than to Simon Cowell.

The two strongest claimants were Robert the Bruce

the elder and John Balliol (1250–1314) and Balliol won, narrowly, on the grounds that his grandmother was William I's brother's *elder* daughter while Bruce's mother was William I's brother's *younger* daughter. Balliol's father, John de Balliol, was the founder of Oxford University's Balliol College, but his claim to the throne came through his mother who cheered John on enthusiastically through all the auditions and heats.

You Win Some, You Lose Some: It's The Wearing Of The Face Paint That Counts

WALES

Scotland and Wales have much in common: they are on the same island; they were both settled by the Celts; they both have towns that begin with 'Aber'; they play each other at rugby once a year; they both voted 'yes' in referenda on devolution in 1997 – and they both suffered terribly at the hands of Edward I.

There are also significant differences between Scotland and Wales. Scotland is known throughout the world for whisky, tartan, kilts, soldiers with kilts, haggis, bagpipes, soldiers with bagpipes and Sean Connery. Wales is not known for any of these things.

Edward I (r1272–1307) was credited with introducing the English parliamentary system and was called Edward the Lawmaker. He also spent the first part of his reign conquering the Welsh, stripping the Welsh princes of their titles and forcing Wales to become part of the Kingdom of England. However, on his death Edward I was given the name Hammer of the Scots and not Hammer of the Welsh, which was an early sign that for the next 700 years Wales would be completely forgotten about.

THE AULD ALLIANCE

In 1295 Edward demanded that Scotland join England in war against France. King John Balliol refused and Scotland, instead, negotiated a separate treaty with the French. This was the beginning of the Auld Alliance of political understanding between the two countries that would last, off and on, until 1565 – and to this day it is fondly remembered in Scotland but completely forgotten about in France, other than in the Auld Alliance pub in Paris.

As you might imagine Edward was somewhat put out by this disloyalty of Scotland and Balliol and proceeded to invade Scotland, sack Berwick, defeat the Scots at Dunbar, take Balliol prisoner and take control of Scotland rendering it an English colony under the charge of a Governor. In an early sign of the many difficulties that the Auld Alliance would encounter over the next 260 years, the French did not come to Balliol's aid.

Nevertheless, Scottish soldiers would fight for the French against the English occupiers in the early 15th century. A Scottish regiment, the Army of Scotland, served in France from 1419–29 when, much like the Tartan Army more than 500 years later, there were victories, there were defeats, there were good times and bad times, much drunkenness and occasional accommodation and transport problems.

THE TAKING OF THE STONE

Edward I's revenge on Scotland included making raids on the country's churches and palaces in search of historic relics which he relocated to England; the most famous of these was Scotland's most sacred and iconic national symbol, the Stone of Destiny at Scone Abbey. Edward's removal of the Stone in 1296 could safely be said to have been provocative.

BRAVEHEART

The five films nominated for Best Picture at the 1995 Academy Awards were by Hollywood standards a strange selection. There was *Sense and Sensibility* – a

Ye Olde English costume drama directed by a man from Taiwan; *Babe* – an Australian fantasy about a talking piglet who wants to be a sheepdog; *Il Postino* – an Italian-language film, about a village postman; *Apollo 13* – which starred Tom Hanks who had already won Oscars in the previous two years so wasn't allowed to win again. And the fifth contender for the gong? An epic about a 13th-century Scottish revolutionary, starring and directed by an apparently slightly deranged Australian and filmed mainly on location in Ireland. The revolutionary was William Wallace, the film was called *Braveheart* and Mel Gibson's Scottish accent was not that bad.

Braveheart was a huge success worldwide and, unsurprisingly, no less so than in Scotland. The film's blue face paint, gruesome violence and all-pervading anti-Englishness stirred the souls of Scots who joined in the shouts of 'freedom' and were inspired to buy Proclaimers albums.

WILLIAM WALLACE

Braveheart the movie also reignited interest in Scotland's greatest martyr, William Wallace (1270, or thereabouts–1305). Wallace was neither a royal prince nor a prominent noble and hardly anything is known about his early life. He was the younger son of a minor landowner, was probably born near Paisley, was well educated and by most accounts he was very tall. Wallace came to prominence in 1297 when he killed the English Sheriff of Lanark, which according to the legend was in revenge for the Sheriff having murdered his young wife Marion, who in the film *Braveheart* was called Murron so that audiences did not get confused with Robin Hood's Marion.

Now an outlaw and on the run, Wallace led an army of rebels that would use guerrilla tactics to attack the English occupiers, causing as much death and destruction as possible. In response, Edward waged upon him a 13th-century version of today's War on Terror by sending an army to Scotland, but Wallace defeated them at Stirling Bridge (1297), where he introduced the tactic – much repeated in World War II films – of waiting until the opposition got onto a bridge before attacking them.

The victory at Stirling Bridge saw Wallace appointed Guardian of Scotland and for a year he successfully continued attacking the English occupiers and raiding the border. A year later however, the English returned and defeated Wallace at Falkirk in 1298. Wallace went into hiding and avoided capture for seven years. Some believed that he lay low in France, but the story of Wallace having an affair with the future queen of England and being the true father of Edward III of England is considered unlikely due to Edward being born seven years after Wallace died.

In 1305 Wallace was betrayed and captured by the English. He was taken to London where he was tried for treason, found guilty and then executed in the most brutal and public way that Edward I could think of: being hanged, drawn and quartered was only the half of it. Wallace was decapitated and his head stuck on London Bridge; four other body parts were then displayed in Newcastle upon Tyne, Berwick, Stirling and what is now Perth, as a grisly reminder not to mess with Edward. In Scotland, Wallace's death confirmed Edward as the Hammer of the Scots and villain of Scottish history, while elevating Wallace to the status of martyr and national hero.

ROBERT THE BRUCE

The Robert the Bruce who became King Robert I (1274–1329) was the grandson of the Robert the Bruce who had been runner-up to John Balliol in the Scottish king competition of 1292. The younger Bruce had at different times been for and against Wallace and for and against Edward I, but he was consistent in seeking the crown that had been denied his grandfather.

In 1306 Bruce met Sir John Comyn in a Dumfries Church – Comyn was his main rival both for the throne and as leader of the Scottish nobles. An argument ensued, weapons were drawn and Comyn was killed – an early example of West of Scotland knife crime. Realising that murder in a church was not the best career move of all time, Bruce decided to stop prevaricating and one month later had himself crowned king at Scone in a ceremony boycotted by the Scottish nobles and with the English still in overall control.

THE SPIDER

The new king soon had to flee for his life, leaving his wife, daughter and sisters in prison while he hid in a cave on tiny Rathlin Island off the Antrim coast of Ireland. With all apparently lost, The Bruce was to take inspiration from a spider which, for hour after hour, tried and failed to spin a web but never gave up, before finally being squashed by Bruce as the spider was doing his head in.

The story of Robert the Bruce and the spider became one of the most famous in Scottish history. Not only did it encourage The Bruce to keep going when all seemed lost, but it also taught the Scottish king that with the great power of the crown came great responsibility, an ethos that would be followed by another Spiderman many centuries later.

The Bruce soon followed William Wallace's example and led guerrilla attacks on the occupying English. Once more, an exasperated Edward I was forced to come to Scotland to quell this latest uprising – this time in 1307, but the elderly king died in July on the Scottish border, with the last thing he ever saw being the Scottish hills in the distance and the last thing he ever heard being the sound in the distance of the Scots singing 'cheerio, cheerio, cheerio'.

BANNOCKBURN

The new English king Edward II (1284–1327) was neither the leader nor soldier that his father had been and this enabled Robert the Bruce to establish his position as King of Scotland and to recapture land and castles until only Stirling remained – under siege but in English hands. An agreement was made in 1313 between Edward Bruce, brother of Robert and the English governor of Stirling Castle that, unless an English army was sent to relieve it, the castle would be surrendered twelve months hence.

With all of Europe watching, Edward II had no alternative and in June 1314, just after Midsummer's Day and Van Morrison's first ever Glastonbury appearance, he took an army across the border and headed towards Stirling; Edward's army comprised more than 15,000 men, The Bruce had just over 6,000. The two armies met for the first time on 23 June at Bannockburn, three miles from Stirling, near Tillicoultry. The battle was over almost before it began. The Scottish king had allowed himself to become separated from his army and, before a single order had been issued, an English knight, Sir Henry de Bohum, charged at him with a lance – but he'd underestimated how small The Bruce's horse was, enabling Bruce to duck and kill de Bohum with one blow.

The early skirmishes were indecisive and, given the overwhelming number of men his army was up against, even into that first night The Bruce was still considering whether to withdraw. But he was persuaded by his colleagues that the English were not united, that their morale was poor and, crucially, that Edward had positioned men with heavy weaponry and armour on the low, boggy ground near the Bannock Burn. The Scots had the advantage of being both less heavily armoured and of being on the higher, drier ground.

The battle began again after dawn on 24 June and was all over by lunchtime, the Scots' infantry with their long spears pressing down and backed by archers, so that the English found themselves hemmed in on poor ground, the fact that there were so many of them now working to their disadvantage, until finally they were forced to break ranks and retreat from the battlefield with the Scots in pursuit.

Edward had to flee the battle in order to evade capture, finally losing his pursuers at Dunbar where, after purchasing some shortbread as presents for the family, he caught a ship back to England.

FLOWER OF SCOTLAND

For Scotland, the events of 1314 ensured national independence and the Battle became a symbol of a proud people, a tenet of faith in times of trouble and commemorated by the building of several housing estates in the Bannockburn area.

The events of Bannockburn would also be commemorated many years later in the lyrics of Scotland's unofficial national anthem *Flower of Scotland*, which was written by Roy Williamson of the Corries in 1967. *Flower of Scotland* was first sung as a sporting national anthem by the British Lions rugby team on their tour of South Africa in 1974, then, by the Scottish rugby team in 1990, in the same year as Scotland famously beat England at Murrayfield to win the Grand Slam, with the Scottish football team following suit in 1993.

The most famous lines in the song, and in many cases the only lines that supporters can remember, concern how proud King Edward II after the Battle of Bannockburn was sent homeward 'tae think again'. We do not know exactly what Edward's emotions were at being the only English leader in all of history to contrive to lose an important battle to the Jocks – and with more than twice the number of men – but it is probably fair to say that thinking again was somewhat of an understatement.

ROSSLYN CHAPEL

A footnote to this period in Scottish history was that the Battle of Bannockburn took place two years after the legendary Knights Templar had been brutally suppressed by the Pope for crimes of heresy in 1312. [For the Templars who were able to escape, some fled to Scotland for safety: due to Bruce's killing of Comyn, Scotland was not only not recognised by the Church, but the whole country had been excommunicated for its king's crime, making any Papal decrees against the Templars irrelevant.] The Knights Templar were extremely wealthy and were renowned for possessing relics of great religious importance. It was believed that some of these relics were taken to Scotland for safe keeping after 1312 and it is said that some Knights Templar fought for The Bruce at Bannockburn.

Rosslyn Chapel, a few miles south of Edinburgh, was founded in the 15th century by a Templar family, the St Clairs of Orkney. The chapel is full of religious and Masonic symbolism and featured in Dan Brown's novel *The Da Vinci Code* published in 2003 and the eponymous film – starring Tom Hanks – released in 2006. Many amazing theories have been offered as to what might have been buried by the Templars underneath Rosslyn Chapel, ranging from the Holy Grail to Tom Hanks' mullet.

DECLARATION OF ARBROATH

Although by the summer of 1314 Scotland's borders were now secure, neither the country's independence nor Robert the Bruce's position as king had been acknowledged by either England or Rome. On 6 April 1320, Scotland's nobility and churchmen put their names to an open letter to Pope John XXII, penned (probably) by the Abbot of Arbroath Abbey – who was also Scotland's most famous Bernard – Bernard de Linton. De Linton's missive became known as the Declaration of Arbroath and a challenge to the world to accept the right of Scotland to be a nation and included the famous lines:

'It is in truth not for glory, nor riches, nor honours that we are fighting, but for freedom . . .' (with emphasis on saying freedom very loudly indeed)

and

'. . . for so long as but a hundred of us remain alive, never will we on any conditions be brought under English rule.'

And the less famous line:

'If our numbers fall below a hundred we will happily give up and agree to stay in sheltered housing.'

The Declaration of Arbroath was also unique in expressing the right of the Scottish people, and not the Scottish king, to independence implying that Robert The Bruce ruled only by the Scottish people's grace. The letter must have had some influence on the Pope for in 1324 the Church of Rome finally recognised The Bruce as king, although he remained excommunicated.

It was not until 1328 and the joint Treaties of Edinburgh and Northampton that England accepted Scottish independence. Robert The Bruce died a year later having finally seen his goal of a free, sovereign nation achieved.

FOOD

Arbroath would find additional fame as the home of the Arbroath Smokie – a headless, gutted haddock that is lightly salted and then hot smoked over hardwood to give the Smokie its distinctive taste. The Smokie is just one of many traditional Scottish delicacies that have become renowned around the world.

The Forfar bridie is a horseshoe-shaped meat pie that originated in the town of Forfar in Angus and it is believed was created as a treat for the lucky bride to be on her wedding day. Another meat-based delicacy is the famous Scotch pie that has a filling of mutton encased in a pastry crust. It has been long associated with Scottish football where traditionally fans attending matches will buy the Scotch pie to throw at the referee.

Scots are also known for having a sweet tooth or

three. Scottish tablet has been made in Scotland for centuries, it is a hard and sweet confectionery made from sugar, condensed milk and butter. Shortbread are biscuits made from a short dough of sugar, butter and either oatmeal or flour, which traditionally was the dough left over when making bread. Shortbread has a crumbly texture and is made into different shapes of rounds or rectangular fingers, or triangles that are given the name of petticoat tails because their pattern and shape resemble a petticoat.

Mince and tatties became a 20th-century staple for many Scots as both an evening meal and a popular school dinner. Many Scottish women would take great pride in their own family recipe and would happily talk mince on a regular basis.

THE BRUCE'S HEART

Immediately after Bannockburn, The Bruce continued his fight against the English, but this time in Ireland, with his brother Edward Bruce invading in 1315 and being declared king of Ireland in 1316, although this Bruce Celtic Empire was to be short-lived with Edward killed in 1318 in Dundalk, even then never the most peaceful of towns.

Robert The Bruce died in 1329, but had one goal that he had not been able to achieve – which was to go on a Crusade to the Holy Land. He left instructions for one of his closest friends, James Douglas, to carry his heart in a casket to the Holy Land. However, Douglas and his followers only got as far as Spain, where in 1330 outside Seville they were killed in battle after a dispute over a sun lounger got out of hand, and Bruce's heart was brought back to Scotland where it was safely buried at Melrose Abbey.

DAVID II

The rest of the 14th century was not kind to Scotland. After The Bruce, Scotland was led by a series of ineffectual leaders. David II (1324–71), the young son of The Bruce, was only four when his father died. The English now had a new more effective king, Edward III, and Edward Balliol, son of John, was determined to reclaim the Balliol right to the Scottish throne. With The Bruce Crown once more in dire straits, it was the French who came to Scotland's aid in 1336 by threatening war on England as part of the Auld Alliance, which saved Scotland, but sparked the beginning of the Hundred Years War between England and France, which as the French pointed out was a little bit of an overreaction.

In 1346 David II led a Scottish army into England, but at Neville's Cross in Northumberland emulated

William the Lion by not only being defeated, but also managing to get himself captured. David II was held prisoner for eleven years before being ransomed back to Scotland in 1357 where he reigned until 1371 when he died without an heir.

The first Scottish parliaments had sat in the 13th century, but they were infrequent gatherings with little real power and it was not until the time of David II's captivity that parliament sat on a more regular basis as they had to find ways of raising taxes to pay for his ransom, so beginning the long tradition of public antipathy towards politicians.

THE BLACK DEATH

As much as a third of Scotland's population had died from the Black Death of bubonic plague in 1349–50 and the subsequent smaller outbreaks that occurred during the 14th century. That England had suffered if anything even more from the Plague and was so embroiled in the Hundred Years War with France that they did not take advantage of Scotland being there for the taking, was as far as Scotland was concerned not much of a consolation.

The Black Death was spread around the country by vermin, and the colder climate and less densely populated Highlands were comparatively unscathed compared to the Lowlands. However, for all Scots the prospect of plagues was their greatest threat in the second half of the 14th century, as movingly described in the UB40 song – 'There's a rat in mi kitchen, what am I gonna do?'

If In Doubt
Call Him James

THE FIRST STEWARTS

David II was succeeded first in 1371 by his nephew
Robert II – grandson of Robert the Bruce and son of
Marjorie Bruce and Walter Stewart, 6th Hereditary
Steward of Scotland – who became the first Stewart
monarch, and then by Robert II's son, Robert III in
1390. Scotland had become a poor, lawless and violent
country and Robert III was an especially ineffective
monarch, ceding real power to his younger brother as
the Douglas and Stewart families fought both each
other and among themselves to gain power and
influence. At least Robert III had the self-knowledge

to realise that he was not much good at being king, as well as being something of an eco-warrior by suggesting that on his death he should be buried on a dung heap

JAMES I

The first King James was James I (1394–1437) who became king, nominally, in 1406 but unfortunately – despite being sent to France to keep him safe – was captured by the English and spent the obligatory period in captivity before returning to Scotland, eighteen years later, in 1424. Determined to make up for lost time James dealt ruthlessly with his lawless nobles and unruly church to reestablish the rule of the Crown. However, James I was not ruthless enough and in 1437 he was lured to a dinner party in Perth where he was stabbed to death, despite the brave attempts to save him by Catherine Douglas, a lady-in-waiting, who used her bare arm as a bolt to stop the assassins from breaking down a door, which as well as being ultimately unsuccessful also ended her badminton career.

The death of James I was to be the first of a series of unfortunate ends to befall the Stewart kings – not dissimilar to Spinal Tap drummers. James II died in 1460 when he was unfortunately blown up while standing too close to a cannon that exploded. And after losing the battle of Sauchieburn in 1488 James III died – possibly killed by rebel soldiers, or died from wounds inflicted when falling from his horse in an attempt to flee, or was stabbed to death by an unknown assailant impersonating a priest, or some combination of the three.

THE THISTLE

It was during the reign of James III that the thistle's status as a royal symbol and national flower of Scotland was established when it appeared on Scottish coins. In 1687 The Order of The Thistle was established with a statutory foundation to reward Scottish peers who supported the king's religious and political aims and today consists of the monarch and sixteen knights and ladies. The motto of the Order is 'Nemo me impune lacessit' or in English, 'No one harms/provokes me with impunity' or as it is officially translated into Scots, 'What yer looking at, ya bas'.

No matter how fitting, it is unclear why the prickly thistle was chosen to be Scotland's national emblem, although legend has it that in the run-up to the Battle of Largs in 1263 a surprise night attack by King Haakon's army on Alexander III's Scots was foiled when the Norsemen, who had removed their footwear so that they would not be overheard, unluckily found themselves barefoot in the dark in a large field of thistles.

BERWICK

In 1482 the Scottish Royal burgh of Berwick-upon-Tweed fell into English hands. This was not in itself an unusual occurrence as after Edward I sacked the town in 1296, it changed nationality between England and Scotland more than a dozen times.

During the 13th century, Berwick had been Scotland's largest and wealthiest town, trading with England, Europe and beyond. After 1482 Berwick remained firmly in English hands, although in a legalistic quirk the town was officially declared to be *of* the Kingdom of England rather than actually being *in* it. Therefore, every time that England or Britain declared war on somebody, Berwick-upon-Tweed had to be specifically mentioned. This was to cause some consternation in 1966 when it was discovered that Berwick was still officially at war with Russia, 104 years after the conclusion of the Crimean War. A Russian diplomat was sent to Berwick with a few cases of vodka and a Russo-Berwick peace treaty was negotiated sometime in the morning.

Although technically English, the county of Berwickshire remained under Scottish control and the local football team Berwick Rangers joined the Scottish League in which they have proudly come bottom for many years. The town itself had made little attempt to return to Scotland until a poll in 2008 showed a majority of its population voting to be Scottish again, with the patriotic prospect of free personal care for the elderly proving the deciding issue.

PIRACY

The Roman word *Scotti*, from which the word Scot comes, also translates as pirate, a translation the Scots would live up to many times over the centuries. As trade from the ports of eastern Scotland with the Netherlands, Scandinavia, Germany and the Baltic States increased so, too, did Scottish piracy, which became so bad that Scots were officially banned in the 15th century from some of Europe's major ports. In response, the Scots would hang about outside the harbour where they would consume extra-strong drink, shout abuse, and moon as many passing ships as possible.

JAMES IV

Throughout the 15th century Scotland had become a nation of powerful families, such as the MacDonalds, the Campbells and the Gordons in the North and the Douglases and the Grahams in the South either fighting each other or joining forces to fight the Stewart kings. It was not until James IV (1473–1513) became king in 1488 that the nation was consolidated firmly under the rule of the Scottish Crown with James taking the title and lands of the Lords Of the Isles. James IV was Scotland's renaissance prince: he expanded Scotland's navy, was an able soldier, built the Palace of Holyrood in Edinburgh in 1501 and supported the arts and education.

The Hundred Years War had finally ended, seventeen years late, in 1453, but the Auld Alliance continued and the early part of James IV's reign saw him in conflict with England, but 1503 saw a change with his wedding to Margaret Tudor (1489–1541), the daughter of Henry VII of England and the sister of the future Henry VIII (1491–1547). This marriage of the Thistle and the Rose not only united the royal families of Scotland and England but also resulted in something of a lifestyle change for James who already had several mistresses and illegitimate children. His most recent paramour, Margaret Drummond, would die suddenly in mysterious circumstances apparently after eating a dodgy breakfast – an early indication of the perils of eating last night's kebab the morning after.

FLODDEN

James IV's marriage to Margaret did not however prevent him taking the disastrous decision to declare war on his brother-in-law, Henry VIII, in support of the French. James raised an army of 20,000, the largest Scottish army ever assembled, and met 20,000 English at Flodden Field in Northumberland in 1513. James was a brave and able soldier and insisted on leading his men from the front where he was only feet away from his English counterpart, the Earl of Surrey, when he was struck down. Unsurprisingly the Scots lost heart after this setback and were driven back and eventually decimated, with more than 5,000 men and most of their nobility killed in what was arguably the worst military defeat in Scotland's history. The song *Flowers of the Forest* is a lament for the fallen of Flodden.

BATTLES

Not only did Scotland have an unenviably bad record when it came to winning battles, but they also had a habit of losing their king in the process. The Battle of Flodden and the death of James IV in 1513 was but one of a long line of bad career moves by Scottish monarchs. Duncan I died after the Battle of Pitgaveney near Elgin in 1040 and the man who defeated him, Macbeth, was himself killed at the Battle of Lumphanan in Aberdeenshire in 1057. Malcolm III was killed at the Battle of Alnwick in Northumberland in 1093. David II was not killed at the Battle of Neville's Cross near Durham in 1346, but was captured by the English and held prisoner for eleven years. James III was killed, probably by his own men, after the Battle of Sauchieburn near Stirling in 1488. And James V died a few days after his defeat at the Battle of Solway Moss in 1542.

Of all the many battlegrounds in Scotland, Falkirk has the dubious honour of having hosted not one, but two major battles: in 1298 a Scottish army led by William Wallace was defeated by the English, and in 1746 Bonnie Prince Charlie's Jacobites defeated the royal troops of George II. Falkirk has remained relatively peaceful since then but when the Queen opened the Falkirk Wheel in 2002 she looked understandably wary.

UNIVERSITIES

James IV was a firm believer in the importance of education and by 1495 Scotland could boast three universities: St Andrews, Scotland's first university, was founded in 1413 with Glasgow founded in 1451 and Aberdeen in 1495. The University of Edinburgh followed in 1582 and Scotland built up an international reputation for further education that has continued to this day, with Edinburgh, St Andrews and Glasgow universities featuring in the top one hundred in the world .

The 20th century saw a plethora of new Scottish universities including Strathclyde and Glasgow Caledonian in Glasgow, Heriot-Watt and Napier in Edinburgh, Dundee and Abertay in Dundee, Robert Gordon in Aberdeen and Stirling and Paisley in Stirling and Paisley respectively. This is not forgetting the numerous Scots of a certain age who will grumble that they are in fact graduates of the University of Life.

EDINBURGH

The largest medieval towns in Scotland by the 14th century were Dunfermline, Berwick, Roxburgh, Perth, Edinburgh, Stirling and Aberdeen. Dunfermline in Fife became Scotland's principal city during the reign of Malcolm III and Margaret in the 11th century and was succeeded in the 13th century by Perth through until 1437. Perth was only two miles from Scone Abbey and the Stone of Destiny and was where the Royal Court was most often to be found.

The murder of James I of Scotland in 1437 saw Perth fall out of favour with the Stewarts and in 1470 Edinburgh, then Scotland's largest city, became Scotland's most important Royal centre and, with that, the country's capital. It was not, however, until after the Union of the Crowns in 1603 and the building of Scotland's first dedicated hall for parliament and the courts in 1639 that Edinburgh was officially given the title capital of Scotland, ironically even though the king and Royal Court had left to live in a completely different country.

During the 14th century Edinburgh and the Port of Leith boasted Scotland's largest population and had become the country's principal centre of trade. The world famous Edinburgh Castle first became a royal residence during the 11th century and the first Palace of Holyroodhouse was built by James IV – on the existing site – in 1501. The road linking the Castle and the Palace was the High Street, which was given the name the Royal Mile in the 16th century. St Giles' Cathedral on the High Street was first built in the

12th century, with current-day interiors dating from the 14th century and after the Reformation also became known as the High Kirk of Edinburgh. On either side of the High Street thousands of people lived in the closes and tenements which lead down to Cowgate and the Grassmarket which lies below the castle. The Grassmarket is famous for having a large number of pubs and has been promoting binge drinking since at least the 16th century.

STIRLING

The other strategic location in Scotland was Stirling. The military garrison at Stirling Castle was at the very centre of the Wars of Independence during the 13th and 14th centuries, although the castle we see today was built in the 16th century with the Great Hall completed in 1503. However it was not until 2002 that Stirling was finally officially declared a city and celebrated with the Thistle Shopping Centre staying open until eight o'clock in the evening.

CASTLES

Edinburgh and Stirling are Scotland's two most visited castles but there are numerous others dotted around Scotland, all shimmering in beautiful orange and purple hues (or that's what they look like in the postcards) and with buttered scones and strawberry jam available from their tearooms.

Blair Castle in Perthshire is not, as you might imagine, Tony and Cherie's holiday home but the ancient seat of the Dukes of Atholl – the Murray family hold the title Duke of Atholl today – and dates from the 13th century. Castle Stalker is a tower house built by the Stewarts in the 14th century on an islet on Loch Laich in Appin, Argyll. Dunnottar Castle as we see it today is a ruin that was built on a rocky headland near Stonehaven, Aberdeenshire, dating back to the time of the Picts. Following the coronation of Charles II at Scone in 1651, the Honours of Scotland (Scotland's Crown Jewels) were taken from Scone to Dunnottar in an attempt to keep them out of Oliver Cromwell's hands. In addition, Dunnottar was one of the locations used in Franco Zeffirelli's 1990 film *Hamlet* – with Mel Gibson smoking the cigar.

One of the most photographed and filmed castles in Scotland is the dramatic Eilean Donan Castle, built and rebuilt since the mid-13th century on an island in Loch Duich near Kyle of Lochalsh. And on Loch Ness, 13th-century Urquhart Castle, a ruin since 1692, is very popular with visitors – not because of its imposing architecture and dramatic history as an important Highland fortress, but just for the opportunity to see if Nessie and family happen to pass by. There are more than 200,000 visitors to Urquhart Castle every year, which does make you wonder how many would come if Nessie actually existed.

GHOSTS

Scottish castles are also renowned for being haunted and more than one hundred of them have reported sightings of spectres and other apparitions and phenomena that cannot be explained in the normal course of events; Culzean, Cawdor, Craigievar, Dunstaffnage, Glamis and Inveraray are but a smattering of those with a resident ghost or two. Scotland's most common ghostly apparitions are invariably either a piper or a woman wearing a green or grey dress, which does make you wonder if there are two ghosts traveling the country for all eternity with the only real excitement being what colour of outfit the lady ghost will decide to wear this evening.

Edinburgh is especially famous for being haunted, to the extent that several organised ghost tours operate around the narrow streets and closes of the Old Town and the Royal Mile. The Royal Mile also hides a warren of closes underground – these were blocked up and the (now) City Chambers was built atop them in 1753 but many of the original streets have been preserved and are now open to the public, much to the chagrin of the resident ghosts who had the place to themselves for more than 200 years.

JAMES V

The reign of James V saw the slow recovery of Scotland after the disaster that was Flodden and another renewal of the Auld Alliance with France. James married the king of France's daughter and then, when she died, he married another French woman, Mary of Guise (1515–60). James V's decision to marry into French royalty put him in conflict with England and his uncle Henry VIII; Henry had hoped James would marry his daughter – and James' first cousin – Mary (who would become, relatively briefly, Mary I, Queen of England).

Until James sought to rekindle close relations with France, Henry VIII had been too preoccupied with his numerous marriages, divorces and beheadings – as well as the small matter of changing the religion of his country – to spend much time bothering with Scotland, but this renewal of the Auld Alliance could not be ignored. Henry tried to persuade James to buy into his policy of Protestantism but was rebuffed. Margaret Tudor, James V's mother and Henry VIII's sister, had done much to keep the two kings on vaguely speaking terms and made sure they sent cards at Christmas, so when she died it was not long before war was declared and the Scots were badly defeated at Solway Moss in Cumbria.

James V took the defeat at Solway Moss extremely badly and when two weeks later, on 8 December 1542, his wife gave birth to his heir, a girl, his depression deepened. 'It began with a lass and it will end with a lass,' he is reported to have said. James V died six days later, aged only thirty, apparently of a broken heart, the final straw being that he was not allowed to call his daughter James.

ROUGH WOOING

The accession of six-day-old Mary (1542–87) as queen of Scotland was too good an opportunity for Henry to miss and he proposed the same idea as Edward I had 150 years earlier; that his son and heir (then as now called Edward) should be promised in marriage to the infant Scottish queen (Margaret then, Mary now), therefore uniting the two kingdoms.

At first the Scots agreed, but then thought better of it. An infuriated Henry sent his army across the border on ever more violent raids to persuade the Scots to agree to the love-match. This tactic would become known as the Rough Wooing, where foreplay included the burning and looting of Edinburgh and the defeat in 1547 of a large Scottish army at the Battle of Pinkie, near Musselburgh, with losses as bad as those suffered at Flodden. This defeat would later be commemorated by Altered Images in their song *Pinky Blue*.

The Wooing continued and only came to an end with the death of Henry in 1547 after one wafer thin mint too many, and the departure of Mary to France in 1548 where she was promised in marriage to the Dauphin Francis, future king of France.

REFORMATION

In his attempt to get out of his marriage to Catherine of Aragon and marry the unfortunate Anne Boleyn, Henry VIII had accidentally turned England into a Protestant country in 1530, and throughout northern Europe support for the Protestant Reformation of the church as espoused by Martin Luther quickly spread. In Scotland, the established Roman Catholic church was seen as being complacent and corrupt and did not help its cause by burning to death Patrick Hamilton – the first Protestant martyr – in 1528. Support for Protestantism grew steadily over the next thirty years, encouraged by the newly Protestant English but also influenced by the teachings and writings of European Protestants such as French theologian John Calvin (1509–64) in Geneva.

When leading Scottish Protestant George Wishart was executed for heresy in 1546, radical Protestants retaliated by murdering Cardinal David Beaton who had authorised the death of Wishart. More and more Scottish noblemen joined the Protestant cause and in 1557 they got together to form the Lords of the Congregation, which became quite a popular Goth rock band of the time.

In 1559 radical Protestant reformer John Knox (1513–72) returned to Scotland from years of exile, imprisonment and lack of shaving. Knox was a follower of John Calvin and had taken on Wishart's mantle as Scotland's most prominent Protestant preacher and was known for his blood-and-death, fire-and-damnation preaching at St Giles' in Edinburgh. Knox wrote *The First Blast of the Trumpet Against the Monstrous Regiment of Women* in 1558 which was meant to be an attack on Mary of Guise, Regent of Scotland and England's Catholic queen, Mary I, but backfired somewhat when Protestant Elizabeth I (1533–1603) succeeded her sister and became queen of England in 1558. Knox's tract also resulted in him no longer being asked to judge the Good Ladies of Edinburgh Home Baking competitions.

Mary of Guise had become regent for her young daughter, Mary Stuart (Queen of Scots), in 1554, but required increasing numbers of French soldiers and military support to sustain her rule. At first she tried to compromise with the Protestant nobles and preachers, but in 1559 decided to march against them, only to be forced back and had to retreat out of Edinburgh to Leith. Negotiations to find a compromise between Crown and the Protestant nobles, who were supported by the English, came to an end when Mary of Guise died in June 1560.

With Queen Mary continuing to live in France, the Scottish parliament with the Protestant lords firmly in charge passed laws banning the Catholic Mass, ending Scottish ties with the Church of Rome, accepting the Protestant Confession of Faith and established the Protestant Church as the only true religion of Scotland. The last Catholic Mass in St Giles' in Edinburgh was sung in March 1560 and John Knox became the first minister of the new Protestant Kirk. In December 1560 the first General Assembly of the new Kirk took place. The Scottish Church was more fundamentally Protestant than the Church of England, giving greater importance to the preaching of the Scriptures and even greater importance to the length of beards. The Scots would tolerate no monarch as head of the Kirk, no royal interference in Kirk affairs and Hell would freeze over before guitars and clapping would ever be allowed. The Church of Scotland was on a mission from God and no mere king or queen would stand its way. In a little more than thirty years Scotland had been transformed from being a Catholic country to a Protestant country and it would remain as such for at least the next 300 years.

MARY

In 1558 Mary, Queen of Scots married the heir to the French throne. In 1559 the Dauphin became King Francis II thus the kingdoms of France and Scotland were united and the Auld Alliance would finally be formalised under one ruler, the king of France. Fifteen fifty-eight also saw the death of the Catholic Queen Mary of England and, as Mary had no children, the throne transferred to her Protestant sister Elizabeth.

Elizabeth was the daughter of Henry VIII and Anne Boleyn but as far as the Catholics were concerned, Elizabeth was illegitimate. The next in line to the English throne and the rightful monarch should have been in fact Mary of Scotland, through her grandmother Margaret Tudor, and the French were quick to state this claim.

It was also around this time that Mary Stewart had begun to spell her royal family name Stuart rather than Stewart – probably to sit more easily with conventional French spelling – and her ancestors happily alternated between the two, much to the annoyance of historians.

If Francis II had lived and if Francis and Mary had had children then Scotland would have become a province of France and, as Elizabeth I died childless, the three kingdoms of England, France and Scotland would have become united under a single monarch. Unfortunately, Francis had always been a sickly child and he died in 1560 aged seventeen with, as far as we know, not even a little royal pleasuring as consolation.

With Scotland now a Protestant nation and Mary of Guise dead, the Treaty of Edinburgh in 1560 expelled the remaining French soldiers from Scotland. Within a year of 'almost' attaining its ultimate goal, the Auld Alliance had formally come to an end and all prospects of Scotland becoming known for gourmet cuisine were lost forever.

MARY AND ELIZABETH

Elizabeth I of England and Mary, Queen of Scots were first cousins and now monarchs of their respective countries. Elizabeth, at 26, was nine years older than Mary but, although they often wrote to each other in the most courteous and loving terms, they did not appear to like each other much and had never met.

With her husband dead there was nothing to keep her in France and Queen Mary, now aged almost nineteen, returned in 1561 to the country she had left when she was five. Mary had refused to sign the Treaty of Edinburgh in 1560 and Elizabeth would not give her safe conduct to travel through England. Mary therefore sailed direct to Scotland where she arrived on a wet day in August. She stayed in Leith for a couple of days, presumably Edinburgh was booked up for the Festival, and the crowds came to take a look at their queen, after all those years of absence. Mary was a nineteen-year-old widow, a devout Catholic, striking in appearance and apparently very tall.

At first things went well. Despite John Knox's attempts to deafen her into converting to Protestantism, Mary remained Catholic but agreed to practise her religion only in private and not to laugh at Knox's beard in public. And other than the odd riot or two Scotland would be remarkably peaceful for the next few years.

LORD DARNLEY

It all went wrong when Mary decided to get married. Elizabeth I of England had been pushing Mary to marry Elizabeth's favourite – and presumed lover – Robert Dudley in a peculiar diplomatic and romantic proposal which none of the three participants actually wanted, but couldn't be seen to say so. Eventually Mary took charge of events by deciding in July 1565 to marry the Catholic Lord Henry Darnley (1546–67) – against the wishes of her nobles, the Church and Elizabeth – and quickly went through with the ceremony before anybody could stop her. Mary was soon pregnant with the all-important heir, but within two years her reign was over.

Mary and Darnley were soon beset by marital difficulties, but rather than seek counselling to work through their issues, or take time out to reflect, both parties opted for more direct action. First, Darnley was involved in the murder of David Rizzio, Mary's loyal Italian secretary, who was forcibly dragged from the queen's private apartments and stabbed to death in the corridor for no other reason than that the queen liked talking to him. In response, and after safely giving birth to their child in 1566 – a boy named James (1566–1625) – it is alleged that Mary was involved in the plot to murder Darnley in February 1567, when the house he was staying in at Kirk o' Field, near Holyrood, was blown up with gunpowder and, just to be on the safe side, Darnley was strangled – his body was found in the garden.

BOTHWELL

Now, Darnley may well have been considered unpleasant, arrogant, a drunkard and not too bright, but murdering him was probably taking things a little too far. Suspicion for the murder immediately fell on James Hepburn, Earl of Bothwell (1535–78), a man with a dangerous reputation who had become Mary's protector.

Bothwell was charged with Darnley's murder, but retaliated by entering Edinburgh with his soldiers, forcing the court to acquit him and then persuading the widowed queen to marry him – which she did in May 1567. In most people's eyes, Mary's acquiescence to the marriage confirmed her involvement in Darnley's death.

The Scottish nobles, after recovering from the shock of all that had happened, decided it was time to put an end to this nonsense and marched against Mary and Bothwell who were forced to flee. The newlyweds parted at Dunbar never to see each other again, and Mary was taken prisoner and forced to abdicate in July 1567 in favour of her one-year-old son, James VI, with Mary's half-brother the Earl of Moray named as Regent on behalf of the infant.

Supporters of Mary have claimed that Bothwell kidnapped Mary and forced her to marry against her will. However, in the remainder of her life with Bothwell, either safely going mad in a Norwegian prison cell or even more safely dead, she made no effort to denounce him and remained consistently vague about the whole episode.

MARY IN ENGLAND

Mary's subjects had rebelled against her but, remarkably, in 1568 Mary escaped from her prison on Loch Leven's island castle by persuading a besotted young guard to set her free and was able to raise a small army of still-loyal supporters, but she was easily defeated by her half-brother Moray at the battle of Langside. With nowhere else to go in Scotland, and facing imprisonment or worse, Mary decided to flee across the border to England in the hope of finding both sanctuary and support from Elizabeth. Having fled, Mary would never again return to Scotland and would never again see her son; she was only twenty-five years old.

Mary remained in England for the rest of her life,

kept under armed guard and moved from one remote castle to the next until she ended up at Fotheringay Castle in Northamptonshire. Throughout the nineteen years Mary was held in England, Elizabeth refused to meet her cousin, and heir to the throne, and hoped only that she would quietly die, or join a nunnery or something. Mary's Catholicism, her claim on the English throne and her inability to stop herself being associated with Catholic plots against Elizabeth made her a constant threat and irritant to her cousin.

Mary living in England was the last thing Elizabeth wanted yet, despite her advisers putting pressure on her to do away with Mary – whose very presence they saw as a clear and present danger – Elizabeth refused to countenance killing her cousin and a fellow monarch. Eventually, however, in 1586 Mary became implicated in the Babington Plot – a conspiracy to assassinate Elizabeth and put Mary on the English throne. Although the Babington Plot was orchestrated by Elizabeth's Secretary of State, Francis Walsingham, in order to entrap Mary, and despite Mary never having supported or approved the idea of murdering Elizabeth, Walsingham ensured that enough mud stuck for Mary to be charged and found guilty of treason.

MARY QUEEN OF SCOTS GETS NECK PAINS

Reluctantly Elizabeth agreed to sign Mary's death warrant and knowing that there was a good chance that the queen might change her mind, her ministers decided that it would be best to get the execution over with as soon as possible. Mary was beheaded on 8 February 1587 in Fotheringay and even then it did not go to plan as it took two or three attempts to remove the head from the body; and after the grisly deed was finally done the executioner proudly held up to the assembled witnesses an auburn wig as the grey-haired head of the Queen of Scots rolled gently along the floor.

So ended the life of Scotland's most romantic and controversial monarch to date. Mary was queen of Scotland and France, and she might have been queen of England; she had continued the Stewart tradition of violent deaths and had begun a new and dangerous trend of Stewarts being executed. Indeed, of all the many, many disastrous reigns by Scottish monarchs throughout history, Mary, Queen of Scots' was probably the most disastrous of all.

Although James VI of Scotland issued a statement of disappointment at his mother's beheading, he was now heir to the English throne, and conveniently a Protestant, and was not about to do anything that might jeopardise his chance to become king of both countries.

Even dead, Mary still caused trouble. Catholic Europe was appalled by Elizabeth's decision to execute a fellow monarch and in 1588, the year after Mary's death, Phillip II of Spain, Elizabeth's brother-in-law, was so keen to return Catholicism to England that he launched the Spanish Armada to lead an invasion on England.

Mary, Queen of Scots was buried at Peterborough in England, but in 1612 with her son James VI doubling as James I of England, her body was exhumed and reburied at Westminster Abbey. Therefore, the two cousins and queens who never actually met in life, ended up just a few feet apart in death, which if nothing else shows that James VI and I had a fairly strange sense of humour.

We Seemed To Have Misplaced Our Monarch

JAMES VI

As with so many Scottish monarchs, the one-year-old James VI had come to the throne at a very early age and was but a pawn in the continuing divisions between the Scottish nobles and intermittent civil war that would break out between rival factions. The young king was brought up at Stirling Castle as a strict Protestant and, although the castle had been deemed the most secure place for him, several attempts were made to capture the young king, culminating in 1582 when sixteen-year-old James was kidnapped and held prisoner for one year in what is now Huntingtower

Castle in Perthshire. When James was finally released he gradually took control of his kingdom, keeping his nobles in check and bringing the Borders and Highlands into line under the Crown.

Elizabeth I had not anointed James as her successor – he was, after all, the son of a woman she had executed – but she hadn't anointed anyone else either and, meantime, her ministers longed for a Stewart succession. On 24 March 1603, Queen Elizabeth I finally died and the following day James VI was proclaimed James I, the new king of England.

So, after centuries of attempts by the English to unite England and Scotland under one sovereign – most noticeably by Edward I and Henry VIII – it was, ironically, a Scottish and not an English king who would finally unify the crowns, with Ireland thrown in on a buy one, get one free offer.

UNION OF THE CROWNS

James VI transferred his entire court to London, took the title James I and called himself Stuart as well as the Scottish Stewart. James was the first to reign this new Kingdom of Great Britain and did so until 1625 during which time he returned to Scotland only once.

Although James' succession to the English throne and his coronation went smoothly, he had to deal with some inevitable opposition. Disappointed by their new king's refusal to tolerate their faith, thirteen English Catholics planned an attack on the king and parliament. This became known as the Gunpowder Plot which sprang into abortive action on 5 November 1605: on the morning of the State Opening of parliament, Guy Fawkes was discovered in the cellars of Westminster, beneath the House of Lords, in close proximity to thirty-six barrels of gunpowder, a fuse, and box of matches. Unsurprisingly the authorities thought this was quite suspicious.

BORDER REIVERS

The Border Reivers was the name given to the English and Scottish raiders who raided the border between England and Scotland for some 300 years up until the 16th century. Known for their ability as horsemen and soldiers, the Reivers were so adept at cattle rustling that even the cows themselves often seemed unaware that they had been kidnapped. The Reivers wore metal helmets which inspired their given nickname, the Steel Bonnets.

Famous Borders' family names include Elliot, Armstrong, Nixon, Thomson, Bell, Johnstone and Jardine. As far as the Crown was concerned, the Borders were a lawless region and it was only when

James VI became king of both England and Scotland in 1603, that the Reivers' power was finally curbed.

During the 17th and 18th centuries many families from the Borders left to settle in Ulster and then later emigrated to America. In 1969, it was a Borderer descendant, Neil Armstrong, who was the first person ever to walk on the moon, although five years later in 1974 another Borderer descendant, Richard Nixon, was the first American President to resign in disgrace.

WITCHCRAFT

Probably the most famous witches in history are the three witches, or three weird sisters, from Shakespeare's *Macbeth* who with their famous prophecies first raised, only to dash Macbeth's hopes of becoming thane of Glamis, thane of Cawdor and even king hereafter. Indeed, with their, 'Double, double, toil and trouble . . .' Shakespeare's witches have given Scottish witches and witches in general a terrible public image that has lasted to this day and real problems in relocating from caves and moving up the property ladder.

Both the Kirk and James VI were obsessed with witchcraft and devil worship. James VI even wrote a book called *Daemonology* about them, suggesting that the more vigilant the monarch, the less likely they were to be harmed by witches. More than 2,000 poor, unfortunate Scottish women were tortured and put to death before the Witchcraft Acts (in force in various forms since the middle ages) were finally repealed in 1736, although Acts concerning witchcraft remained on the statute book until 1951, and Scottish women with long, pointed noses could finally breathe more easily, except in the winter when their sinuses were blocked.

Even after 1735, Scots long retained their belief in witchcraft and the supernatural. Robert Burns wrote of warlocks, witches and Satan in 1790 in *Tam O' Shanter*. Ghost stories were told throughout Scotland, with houses and most castles reckoning to be home to a haunting or two. Indeed, any woman living in Scotland who has toyed with having a herb garden is looked at with suspicion.

These days, however, devil-worship has fallen out of fashion in Scotland, although the 1973 film *The Wicker Man* tells of a Scottish police sergeant, played by Edward Woodward, on a remote, pagan Hebridean island who ends up as a human sacrifice; the islanders chant, 'E-war, Woo-war,' as he burns. E-War Woo-War being of course what you call Edward Woodward if the letter d did not exist

CHARLES I

James and his son Charles (1600–49) were brought up as Protestants but neither of them followed the strictures and doctrines of the Calvinist, Presbyterian Kirk. James VI commissioned an English translation of the Bible – the *King James Bible* – which was published in 1611 from when it evolved over the years as the *Authorised Version*, and this ultimately eclipsed all previous English translations of the Bible. It should be noted that James commissioned this translation in English only, and not in Scots.

Charles I was born in Dunfermline in 1600 and was the last monarch of either Scotland or England to be born in Scotland. Charles succeeded his father and was crowned king of England at Westminster Abbey in 1625 but was not crowned in Scotland until his belated coronation in Edinburgh in 1633 – the first time he'd set foot in the land of his birth since infancy. Charles was as stubborn as his father but nowhere near as politically astute and proceeded to fall out with absolutely everybody.

THE COVENANT

James and Charles both practised the Anglican faith in which the king was head of the church and the church was run by bishops – both kings believed in the Divine Right of Kings: everybody is answerable to the monarch and the monarch is answerable only to God – the Presbyterian Kirk had it that everybody was answerable only to God. Both kings, also, tried to impose the *Book of Common Prayer* on Scotland. In 1637 at St Giles' the Dean of Edinburgh was reading from the *Book of Common Prayer* for the first time when it is claimed that Jenny Geddes, a local woman, threw her stool at him so initiating a general disturbance involving shouting, shoving and dislodging of women's Sunday hats.

This ongoing religious dispute culminated in the National Covenant of 1638 which was a petition presented and signed in front of the Greyfriars Kirk pulpit in Edinburgh. A copy is still on display at Greyfriars today, setting out Scotland's right to have its own church (as long as it was Presbyterian) and Scotland's right to an independent parliament which would support said church (as long as it was Presbyterian). The Covenant received widespread support throughout Scotland and these supporters were called the Covenanters and they raised an army to support their demands and marched into England twice in 1639 and 1640 to prove their point.

CIVIL WAR

If Charles I had problems in Scotland they were relatively minor compared to his problems in England. He fell out with his English legislature to such an extent that he dissolved parliament for the fourth time in March 1629 and only recalled parliament in 1639 when he ran out of money because he needed to raise an army after his defeat at Berwick. Attempts to find common ground between the king and parliament were not successful, and by January 1642, when Charles attempted to forcibly arrest his opponents in the House of Commons, it is safe to say that the relationship had irreconcilably broken down and in August of that year the English Civil War began.

Scotland was divided over which side it might ally with, or whether to stay neutral in the English Civil War. Despite the disputes with the Covenanters since 1638 Charles returned to Edinburgh in 1641 to look for support and, although the Scots were quite happy to send their king back south empty handed, they were less keen that others should be in a huff with him.

Eventually, in 1643, the Covenanters – who had gained a majority in the Scottish parliament – agreed with the English parliament a Solemn League and Covenant (so called because of the lack of the jokes in the document) and offered help and troops to the

Roundheads, but supporters of King Charles rallied around James Graham, the Marquis of Montrose (1612–50) and soon Scotland had its very own civil war.

Graham had been a Covenanter, but had a greater loyalty to his king. In 1644 with an army of Irish and Highlanders he began a campaign in support of Charles that saw him defeat the Covenanters at Tippermuir and Kilsyth, before being defeated in 1645 at Philliphaugh.

The Scottish government army, as well as fighting Royalist supporters in Scotland, had also joined up with the parliamentary forces in England, fighting on the winning side – the parliamentarians – at the Battle of Marston Moor. By 1646 Charles and his Royalists had been defeated conclusively both north and south of the border. Charles decided to surrender to the Scottish army at Newark upon Trent, in the hope that the Scots – increasingly aware that the English were not going to accept Presbyterianism as they had hoped – would be willing to take on an unemployed but fully trained king looking for a kingdom. However, stubborn as ever, Charles refused to sign the Covenant as demanded by the Scots. A period of uncertainty ensued, with disunity between those Covenanters who wanted to engage with the king and those who were opposed to him. Eventually, the principled Scots decided to hand Charles over to the English parliamentarians for the price of £400,000 in 1647.

Even in captivity Charles continued to negotiate to regain power and now came to an agreement with the Scots whereby he would accept the Covenant and would support Presbyterianism in England if they would come to his aid. Charles of course did not mean a word of it, but in 1648 the Scots invaded England on his behalf to start the Second English Civil War, but were defeated by Oliver Cromwell (1599–1658) and his parliamentarian army at the Battle of Preston in August.

The most radical of the Presbyterians came from the south-west of Scotland and in 1648 they had marched on Edinburgh to support the Covenant. They were called Whiggamores because they used the term 'whiggam' to encourage their horses to go faster. The term Whiggamores or Whigs became associated with supporters of the Covenant and would later be applied to those who opposed tolerance of Catholicism in both Scotland and England. During the 18th century, the Whigs became one of two major political groups along with the Tories in Britain and in the mid-19th century would come to be known as Liberals. If you think

Whigs is a strange sort of name for a major political movement, then at least it was better than the alternative the Giddyups.

In January 1649 Charles was charged and tried for high treason. He refused to acknowledge the Court's right to try him but was, nevertheless, found guilty and on 27 January was sentenced to death. On 30 January 1649 at the Palace of Whitehall, Charles I, king of England, Scotland and Ireland, emulated Mary by becoming the second Scottish Stewart monarch to lose their head (although unlike his grandmother it only took one blow to remove his head).

CROMWELL

No matter how untrustworthy Charles I had been towards them, the Scots were still appalled by the execution of their king. His son and heir Charles II (1630–85) came to Scotland in 1650 and, like his father, reluctantly agreed to sign both the National and Solemn Covenant in return for Scottish support to regain his kingdoms on both sides of the border. Oliver Cromwell took his New Model Army to face Charles's Scottish forces at Dunbar in September 1650.

The Battle of Dunbar was another Scottish military disaster with 3,000 killed and 10,000 taken prisoner. Despite having twice the number of soldiers as Cromwell, the Scots were easily defeated after their commanders lost their strategic hill-top advantage and when the Roundheads launched a surprise attack the Scots line quickly broke. Cromwell, who before the battle had been desperately trying to persuade the Scots not to fight at that stage because he feared he would lose, marched into Edinburgh unopposed.

Despite the defeat at Dunbar, Charles II remained in Scotland, was crowned at Scone in January 1651 and raised another Scottish Royalist army, which exactly one year after the defeat at Dunbar was conclusively defeated, again by Cromwell, at the Battle of Worcester on 3 September 1651 – the last battle of the English Civil War.

Cromwell was now in complete control of England and Scotland and proceeded to abolish all Scottish institutions and incorporate Scotland as a mere province in the new English Republican Commonwealth. This situation served as a kind of preview of what the Union would become fifty years later. Scotland under Cromwell was peaceful, although his insistence on tolerance for all religious beliefs was almost too much for the Scottish Kirk to bear and they pined for happier times – when there was persecution, zealotry and general burning in hell of all who strayed from the Presbyterian doctrine.

HONOURS OF SCOTLAND

The Honours of Scotland are the Crown, Sceptre and Sword that make up the Scottish Crown Jewels and are today on display, next to the Stone of Destiny, in Edinburgh Castle. They date from the reigns of James IV and James V and were first used together at the coronation of the very young Mary, Queen of Scots in 1543. The Crown was made from gold mined from Leadhills in Lanarkshire, one of Scotland's highest villages and famous for its mining of gold, lead and silver.

Cromwell was determined to claim and destroy the Honours, as Edward I had the Stone of Destiny, but the Scots took them from Scone, where they had been used for the coronation of Charles II, to Dunottar Castle near Stonehaven. Cromwell's men laid siege to Dunottar in 1652, but on finally breaking into the castle after eight months they found that the Honours had gone, having been smuggled to nearby Kinneff kirk by a local woman who was always wearing fancy crowns and was therefore beyond suspicion.

The Honours were finally brought back to Edinburgh in 1660, only to be locked away again in

1707 after the Act of Union. They were then more or less forgotten about until, along with a long-lost set of house keys and several missing jigsaw pieces, they were hauled out and dusted off in 1818 in time for the Royal visit to Scotland by George IV.

SCOTTISH PARLIAMENT

In 1640 Scotland, finally – it had taken more than 400 years – got around to having its own full-time parliament, which was opened opposite St Giles' Cathedral on the Royal Mile in Edinburgh, which makes the five-year wait for the country's current Holyrood parliament building seem quite swift in comparison. With the Scottish king Charles I long gone it was decided that a procession would take place, to follow the Honours of Scotland from Edinburgh Castle to the new parliament – a symbolic gesture to mark Scotland's independence.

The tradition of the Riding, established during Scotland's old parliament was revived by the new Scottish parliament in 1999 and when the Holyrood parliament building was finally opened in 2004, MSPs and dignitaries followed Queen Elizabeth II on a route down the Royal Mile from Parliament Hall to Holyrood, the less sprightly among them glad that it was downhill all the way.

CHARLES II

In 1660, with Cromwell dead, Charles II of Scotland was restored as king of England, too. He became known as the Merrie Monarch and famed for his hedonistic lifestyle and, not surprisingly, he was never seen in Scotland again. Charles also renounced his previous support for the Scots' Covenant and insisted on bringing back the bishops. Many Covenanter ministers resigned and left their churches, but would continue to preach in secret in houses, barns and in the open air (weather permitting) and were called the Conventicles.

The 1670s saw continued friction between the Covenanters and the official church of the Episcopal Crown. A Covenanter army was defeated at the Battle of Bothwell in 1679 and some 1,200 prisoners were held at Greyfriars Kirkyard, next to the church where the original Covenant had been signed back in 1638. This period was known as the Killing Time with the remaining Covenanters in constant danger of being executed, imprisoned or exiled.

IRELAND

With the Union of the Crowns in 1603 James VI and I also became king of Ireland and throughout the 17th century thousands of Scots emigrated to Northern

Ireland, 1,000 years since the Irish Scots emigrated to Scotland, as part of a government plan to establish Protestant settlements, or 'plantations', in Northern Ireland. The Scots were given land, the native Catholic Irish were forced out and large parts of the south and west of Northern Ireland became Protestant and remain so to this day.

The Ulster Scots seemed to be keen on the idea that travel would broaden the mind and during the 18th century 250,000 of them emigrated to America, and throughout the 19th century many more were to follow their example. When we think of Irish-Americans today, we think St Paddy's Day and Americans of Irish Catholic descent, but it is believed that the majority of Americans with Irish ancestry hail from the Protestant Ulster Scots. Fourteen US Presidents, from Andrew Jackson to Bill Clinton, have Scots-Irish ancestors and anything up to twenty million Americans today are from the same Scots-Irish Protestant heritage as the Reverend Ian Paisley, which might perhaps explain why so many Americans talk very loudly.

JAMES VII

Charles II died in 1685 and was succeeded by his brother James VII (1633–1701) who was, inconveniently, openly Catholic and demanded tolerance of his faith. This was never going to work out, and when in 1688 James' second wife gave birth to a Catholic male heir the English parliament had had enough. In a plan to overthrow their king they began negotiations with his Protestant daughter Mary and her Dutch Protestant husband William of Orange (1650–1702) – who also happened to be the grandson of Charles I – suggesting that the couple become joint monarchs, although at first Mary was to be sole monarch with William merely her consort. In November 1688 William landed in England with a large Dutch army which faced little opposition. The following month, James VII was forced to flee to France leaving William and Mary free in February 1689 to be declared co-rulers of England and Scotland.

Scotland had been sidelined during the major developments of what became known as the Glorious Revolution. But the Scots had grown accustomed to the English deposing Stewart kings and so – while pointing out that it would have been nice to have been asked first – they went along with the Protestant Dutchman becoming their new king.

In 1689 John Graham, Viscount Dundee, raised an army to support the deposed James who had gone to Ireland where he was still recognised as king. (The

Scottish parliament had declared in April 1689 that James had forfeited his crown due to his flight from Britain.) Graham's army was made up of Highlanders who defeated a government force at Killiecrankie on 27 July 1689, but Graham was killed in battle and the first Scottish Jacobite uprising petered out. Graham became immortalised with the moniker Bonnie Dundee – one of the few occasions when those two words were ever used in conjunction with each other.

WILLIAM AND MARY

William followed James to Ireland and defeated him at the Battle of Boyne on 1 July (12 July on the Gregorian calendar) 1690, with James once more being forced to flee and once more to France. James remained in exile until his death in 1701, never having formally abdicated his throne or his right of his heirs to succeed him. William never visited Scotland, but he has become extremely popular as the Protestant hero King Billy whose victory at the Boyne is still celebrated today by the Orange Order marching on 12 July. The Orange Order was formed in 1795. It has around 100,000 supporters in Scotland, including 20,000 in Glasgow alone, and has kept flute-makers in regular employment for centuries.

Interestingly, back in 1688 the events of the

Glorious Revolution were but part of a wider European conflict which saw France at odds with most of the rest of Europe that consisted of a Catholic-Protestant Alliance that included the Netherlands, the Holy Roman Empire and Spain. The Pope was quite supportive of William's invasion as the Church of Rome was in conflict with Louis XIV at the time and the French were supporting James, but this has tended to be forgotten over the centuries.

CHURCH OF SCOTLAND

It is possible that the Scots might have eventually accepted the Episcopalian Church that had been imposed by the 17th-century Stewart kings, but in 1690 William accepted the Scottish parliament's proposal that the country should revert to the Presbyterian kirk and do away with the bishops once and for all. A General Assembly was held for the first time since 1653 and, in return for accepting William and Mary as monarchs, the reformed Presbyterian church was established as the national Church of Scotland and black was definitely back.

GLENCOE

After the first Jacobite uprising in 1689 and concerned about further rebellions that might happen in the still-Catholic Highlands, the government ordered all clan chieftains to swear allegiance to William III by the end of December 1691. Reluctantly, all the chieftains obeyed the order but, due to an administrative error and bad weather, MacDonald of Glencoe was a few days late.

The government decided to make an example of the MacDonalds and sent 120 men to be billeted with the clan at Glencoe. After enjoying MacDonald hospitality for twelve days, the Earl of Argyll's men, under Robert Campbell, were given fresh orders: all the MacDonalds of Glencoe aged under seventy were to be put to the sword. In the early hours of 13 February 1692, Campbell's men set about their task. Three villages were put to the torch, thirty-eight MacDonalds were killed in their beds or as they fled, forty more died of exposure having fled the glen; the only consolation being that those who survived were able to tell the world about the massacre. The massacre did little for relations between the Campbells and the MacDonalds, who had been feuding for centuries, but the real villains were the government, lead by Secretary of State John Dalrymple, who had hatched the plot, and William who had sanctioned the massacre.

DARIEN

From the 12th century onwards, Scottish merchants had been trading with northern Europe and colonisation of America opened up new markets in the New World. When Port Glasgow was built in 1688, Glasgow became a major centre, trading in tobacco, flax and sugar, but had to contend with English customs and excise and fierce competition from English merchants, although England was far and away Scotland's biggest market. Edinburgh was then the largest city in Scotland with more than 30,000 people and life in the increasingly overcrowded Old Town was becoming more and more grim.

In 1695 a successful banker, William Paterson (1658–1719), who had already been one of the founders of the Bank of England a year previously, persuaded the Scottish parliament to set up the Scottish Trading Company in an attempt to emulate the English East India Company and, with the promise of high profits to be made, thousands of Scots invested their savings in the venture. The first and only Scottish colony was Darien in Panama, Central America.

In 1698, 1,200 hopefuls, led by Paterson, left Scotland on five ships and when they arrived in Darien they named it New Caledonia. What they found was an inhospitable, disease-ridden swamp where, and when trade was not being boycotted by English merchants, they were being attacked by the Spanish who claimed control of that part of Panama.

The East India Company, fearing it would lose its monopoly on British trade with the Indies had lobbied parliament and the orders not to do business with Scottish traders had been approved all the way up to King William himself. William of Orange may well have been a hero to Scottish Presbyterians but over Darien he did everything in his power to ruin Scotland's economy – despite being that nation's head of state.

Those who survived the first year on Darien then abandoned the colony, heading east for home across the Atlantic as a second expedition was sailing west towards the now-abandoned colony. By 1700, the Scots had decided to leave Darien for good: 2,000 settlers were dead, thousands of investors were destitute and Scotland was bankrupt. The dream of a Scottish Empire was abandoned, Scotland was humiliated. Although, on the positive side, when the Panama Canal was built in 1914 to connect the Atlantic and Pacific Oceans and transform international shipping, at least Scotland had the consolation of showing that their idea had potential.

Indeed, the early 18th century as a whole was not kind to Scots on the high seas. Captain turned privateer William Kidd (1645–1701) from Greenock was hanged for piracy with his treasure – if there ever was any – undiscovered. And what about Alexander Selkirk (1676–1721) from Fife? He was the unfortunate sailor abandoned for four years on the uninhabited Juan Fernandez islands in the Pacific. He was also the inspiration behind Daniel Defoe's *Robinson Crusoe* – but Selkirk had no Man Friday and had to do all his own ironing.

British And Proud: 'Come On Tim'

ACT OF UNION 1707

The Nation of Scotland ceased to be an independent
state in 1707. In retrospect, it was quite extraordinary
that it had lasted out so long, having survived attempts
by the Romans, the Angles, the Vikings, Edward I,
Henry VIII and the Union of Crowns to unify the
island of Britain as one political entity, but all good
things come to an end.

The Darien disaster had dealt a major blow to the
Scottish economy, to the extent that it needed
propping up. England would give financial help, but
at a price – union of the parliaments.

Queen Mary II died in 1694, William III in 1702 and James VII and II died in exile in 1701. The crown had passed to Mary's sister and James' daughter, Anne (1665–1714), who became – so far – the last ever monarch of an independent Scotland. Neither Mary nor Anne had any heirs, which meant that the only surviving Stewart was James Edward Stewart (1688–1766), the Catholic son of James VII whose birth in 1688 had precipitated the overthrow of his father.

The English parliament had already planned that, on Anne's death, the crown should go to the Protestant Hanoverian family from Germany descended from Elizabeth, daughter of James VI; they did not want Scotland coming up with any alternative suggestions and they certainly did not want a return to the Catholic Stewart line.

Negotiations towards an Act of Union began in 1702, but the two sides were far apart ideologically and it was not until 1705 that talks began in earnest, and then only because England had forced the Scottish hand with the Alien Act. Determined to bring the Scots to the table, the Alien Act stated that unless the Scots accepted parliamentary union, they would lose their rights as equal citizens in the Kingdom of England – and, furthermore, Scotland would be subject to centuries of unexplained aerial phenomena.

On the matter of union, Scotland's parliament was divided into those in favour (which included some of those who were negotiating), those against and those who could be persuaded; the Scottish public was overwhelmingly against.

In 1706, England put forward formal proposals – the Articles of Union. Scotland would retain its own Presbyterian church (which kept the Kirk on side) and legal system; it would have forty-five MPs in the House of Commons and sixteen Scottish Peers would sit in the Lords; English customs and import duty would cease to be levied on the Scots and they could trade freely with the growing English Empire. On the other hand, Scotland would be under the jurisdiction of the parliamentary union in terms of – among other things – taxation, control of the army and navy and the succession of the monarchy.

With a Scottish majority against the proposed union, negotiations were slow to move forward but, one by one, Scotland's MPs were persuaded that there was merit to be gained. This change of heart, coincidentally, came about at around the same time as large amounts of money were being offered by the Queen's High Commissioner James Douglas, Duke of Queensberry (1662–1711) to charities of the MPs' choice.

The Articles of Union were agreed in July 1706 with the Treaty ratified the following year when, on 16 January 1707, the Scottish parliament voted by 110 to 67 to give themselves a 300-year recess. There were demonstrations around Scotland and the good folk of Edinburgh had their annual riot but, otherwise, Scotland accepted the inevitable and on 1 May 1707 ceased to be an independent state.

Of the Act, the Earl of Seafield (who signed as Lord Chancellor) said, '. . . ane end of ane auld sang', Robert Burns wrote, '. . . we're bought and sold for English gold; such a parcel of rogues in a nation!', and the Spice Girls sang, ''cause tonight is the night when 2 become 1'.

JACOBITES

James Edward Stewart, son of James VII and II, who was to be given the nickname the Old Pretender, was at this stage actually quite young and keen to regain the thrones that had been taken from his father. Supporters of both father and son were given the name Jacobites, after the Latin form of James – *Jacobus*.

In 1708, one year after the Act of Union, young

James set off from France with 6,000 soldiers in thirty ships intending to land in Scotland. However, bad weather and sabotage enabled the Royal Navy to chase James into the Firth of Forth and prevent him landing. The invasion had to be cancelled and, with that, the best chance the Jacobites would ever have was lost, although unfortunately nobody realised this at the time. In 1714, when Queen Anne died and the British parliament formally rejected James in favour of his distant German cousin George, the Old Pretender decided to try again.

THE 15

The Jacobite standard was raised by the Earl of Mar at Braemar in September 1715 and 8,000 Highland clansmen responded to the call, but the Lowland and the English Catholics were, at best, ambivalent and nobody seemed to have a plan. When the Jacobites failed to win the Battle of Sheriffmuir in November the Rising was pretty much over. James had yet to leave France, and by the time he finally arrived, several months late, in Scotland – he landed at Peterhead in December – there was nothing much for him to do other than spend some time sightseeing before heading back to France in February 1716 never to return.

ROB ROY

Not all the Scottish clans supported the Jacobites. The Campbells were loyal to the British Crown – their chief, the Duke of Argyll, led forces against the Jacobites – and in 1725 the Black Watch was set up by Major General George Wade as a Highland regiment loyal to King George.

One clan which was not loyal to the British crown, or any crown for that matter, was clan MacGregor. The MacGregors had annoyed James VI to such an extent that in 1603 he not only took their land but also banned the use of MacGregor as a surname. For 200 years the MacGregors were outlaws and rustlers and were referred to as the Children of the Mist – there was a lot of mist in the Highlands at the time. The most famous MacGregor was Rob Roy (1671–1734) who was a second-hand cattle dealer, outlaw and hero of a novel by Walter Scott.

BONNIE PRINCE CHARLIE

Thirty years after the Jacobite rebellion in 1715, Scotland was peaceful. Major General Wade had built a series of garrisons and roads connecting the Highlands to the rest of Scotland and the remaining Jacobites were mostly old men living in exile, nursing a malt and dreaming of midges.

It came as something of a surprise, therefore, when in July 1745 Charles Edward Stewart (1720–88), the twenty-five-year-old Italian-born son of the Old Pretender, arrived on the Isle of Eriskay with seven of his pals. Charles would be given the nickname, the Young Pretender.

It soon became clear that Charles was not planning a summer's holiday sailing on the West Coast, and in August 1745 at Glenfinnan, at the head of Loch Shiel, he raised his father's standard and called for support to restore the Stewarts to the thrones of Scotland and England. By September a Jacobite army had been raised, had defeated the only government army remaining in Scotland at the Battle of Prestonpans and had taken Edinburgh unopposed.

THE 45

Everybody had been taken by surprise by the arrival of the Young Pretender as nobody knew he was coming. Initially, this worked to his advantage but it was soon to work against him. The Highland chiefs were divided – for every clan who enthusiastically supported Charles, another kept its distance – and the rest of Scotland, although curious about having a Stewart prince in their midst after all these years, had no intention of supporting him and hoped he wouldn't stay long. The French, whose support and troops were vital, were not in favour of Charles' plan and were in the huff because they'd not been consulted – even Charlie's dad didn't think it was a good idea.

Charles had fewer men under his command than there had been in the 1715 rebellion, but he marched into England anyway. The British government panicked, briefly, then realising there was nothing to worry about, sent in two large armies against the Jacobites.

Charles marched through Manchester and on to Derby before, in December 1745, he was persuaded to turn back – with his dream of restoring the Stewart monarchy in tatters, a trip to the Lake District brought little consolation.

CULLODEN

The Jacobites retreated into Scotland, pursued relentlessly by George II's son, the Duke of Cumberland (1721–65). Finally, on 16 April 1746 the two armies met at Culloden Moor, near Inverness, in what is to date the last battle to have been fought on British soil.

There were only 5,000 tired, hungry and fed up Jacobites left, compared to 10,000 fresh, well-fed and well-armed British troops. Many of the British troops were, in fact, Scots – indeed, there were more Scots fighting against the Jacobites than for them.

Charles insisted on taking personal command for this final battle and – disastrously – sent his troops up the hill to meet Cumberland's men. On a cold, wet, dreich day, and in a battle lasting little more than an hour, the Jacobites were decimated: they were killed in combat or cut down as they fled, the injured were killed where they lay – Cumberland's men made no attempt to take prisoners. Culloden was a one-sided battle: more than 2,000 Jacobites died on the field and in the days that followed many more were tracked down and executed, although figures vary, government casualties were possibly fewer than 60.

THE BUTCHER

Charles fled the battlefield and spent the next five months criss-crossing the Highlands and Islands, singing songs on the boat to Skye and assuming numerous disguises in order to keep one step ahead of his pursuers. Many Highlanders risked death and shunned the substantial bounty in their willingness to shelter the prince, but it was Flora MacDonald who encouraged Charles to cross-dress by disguising him as her surprisingly tall Irish maid, Betty Burke. Flora was to be imprisoned in the Tower of London but was released in 1747 and lived until 1790 but she was one of the lucky ones.

In September 1746, Charles set sail from Scotland to France – he'd boarded ship with the Redcoats only two miles behind him. He was never to return but, or so the story goes . . . as a parting gift, he left the recipe for a honey-flavoured whisky liqueur called Drambuie, which was nice of him. For the ensuing forty-two years, until his death in 1788, Charles lived in France and Italy, sired no heirs and drank more than was good for him. But he is forever remembered as the Bonnie Prince of 1745.

While Charles became a romantic hero, thousands of Highlanders were dying in his name. The Duke of Cumberland, he who murdered the wounded at Culloden, was ruthless in his pursuit of the Jacobites. Cumberland was the third son of George II but became better known in Scotland as the Butcher – much to the annoyance of the many decent, law-abiding butchers across the country.

In the wake of Culloden martial law was declared in Scotland and Cumberland ordered that any and all suspected Jacobite rebels – including women and children – were shot, hanged or imprisoned. Carrying traditional Highland weapons was banned, as was wearing tartan and speaking Gaelic. Land that had belonged to clan chieftains was taken from them by force and within just a few years the entire clan system – for centuries the mainstay of Highland life – had been systematically dismantled. In retrospect, Charlie should have probably taken his father's advice and stayed at home.

Mendelssohn Fiddles
While Robert Burns

CRIME AND JUSTICE

'If it bleeds it leads' has long been a media maxim, which when applied in Scotland highlights two facts: that there is traditionally a not insignificant number of crimes to report, and that the public have an inordinate interest in finding out more about the villains in their midst.

Scotland has a long and ignoble history in serial killers. It is now believed that the 16th-century mass-murderer and cannibal Sawney Bean did not actually exist. Bean and his wife were said to have hidden for twenty-five years in a cave in Galloway but, as historians have proved, nothing out of the ordinary has ever taken place at any time in Galloway. But the 19th-century mass-murderers, William Burke and William Hare, did, very much, exist.

Originally from Ulster but working as labourers in Edinburgh their job was to supply dead bodies for dissection to Dr Robert Knox's school of anatomy at Surgeon Square in Edinburgh. The fresher the body, the better paid they'd be by Knox, thus Burke and Hare took up murder. In less than one year they had supplied Knox with at least sixteen victims before they were caught and convicted. Burke was hanged in 1829 but Hare was acquitted after giving evidence against Burke and fled to England.

The Scottish legal system, along with education and the church, remained independent of England even after the Act of Union. The Court of Session was retained as Scotland's highest civil court with, at local level, the Sheriff Court dealing with more minor matters (the High Court of Justiciary is today's supreme criminal court). Scotland has advocates while England has barristers, Scotland has a procurator fiscal while England has a public prosecutor.

Scottish law also has the controversial 'not proven' verdict available to juries. Historically, in Scotland verdicts were either proven or not proven – in

England, guilty or not guilty – but after the Act of Union, the use of 'guilty' and 'not guilty' became more popular in Scotland. The 'not proven' verdict has been kept, however, as a means of expressing that the defendant probably did it, but the prosecution have not proved it, or that the defendant definitely did it, but is a bit scary and knows where we live.

The not proven verdict, has been termed the bastard verdict, and was most infamously applied in the case of Madeleine Smith in 1857 who was 'not proven' to have poisoned her lover – even though the police found her with a very large bottle with a skull and crossbones and the word POISON on it.

In recent years Scottish crime has found international fame through the long-running STV drama *Taggart*. A detective series set in Glasgow, *Taggart* was first screened in 1983 and has become legendary for making the phrase 'there's been a murder' one that can only now be said in a Scottish accent.

BANKING (PART ONE)

Scottish-born William Paterson, of Darien infamy, was a key founder of the Bank of England in 1694; a year later the Bank of Scotland was set up in Edinburgh. The Royal Bank of Scotland was also later established in Edinburgh, in 1727, and both the Bank and the

Royal enjoyed significant expansion during the 18th century, alongside the growth of the Scottish economy post-Union.

The Act of Union of 1707 opened trade links between the colonial New World and Scotland; Glasgow – ideally placed on the west coast – rivalled Edinburgh as a major centre of trade. Numerous banks sprung up in the west of Scotland, but it was the Clydesdale Bank, founded in 1838 in Glasgow and named after the geographical area rather than a large horse, that was to prove to be the longest lasting.

The Clydesdale was sold to the English Midland Bank in 1920 and then again to the National Bank of Australia in 1987, but retained its presence in Scotland. Along with the Bank of Scotland and the Royal Bank of Scotland, it continued to print Scottish notes, much to the annoyance of generations of English shopkeepers and London taxi-drivers.

The Bank and the Royal remained at the very centre of Scottish life until 2001 when the Bank of Scotland merged with the Halifax Building Society to form a new group called HBOS. At first it seemed that life would carry on as normal for worried Scottish customers who had been with the Bank of Scotland all of their lives, but it soon became clear that behind the jovial, singing and dancing persona of the Halifax front man, Howard Brown, was a calculating mastermind who was determined to see power transferred south of the border.

The Royal had always been a little posher than the Bank of Scotland, and are credited with being the first bank in the world to offer customers, or the more exclusive of their customers anyway, an overdraft facility, and would not have dreamed of merging with a mere building society. The Royal Bank saw great expansion at the end of the 20th century, to the extent that it was not only the wealthiest company in Scotland, but was the sixth largest bank in the world. Happy days.

JAMES HUTTON

James Hutton (1726–97) from Edinburgh instigated the basis of modern geological theory and wrote about it in his world-changing book about how the world changed in *Theory of the Earth* published in 1788. From his experiments while farming in Berwickshire and studies of the volcanic rock that is Arthur's Seat in Edinburgh, Hutton deduced that different layers and types of rock signified different periods in time. The Earth, he concluded, was much, much older than we had thought it was, and certainly older than the 6,000 years stated in the Bible.

Hutton's theories would be developed in the 19th

century by the geologist Charles Lyell, (1797–1875) from Angus, who questioned still further the accepted view – divine creation – of life on earth. Some of Lyell's findings would, in turn, both encourage and influence Charles Darwin as he developed his theory of evolution by natural selection. From 1825, at the age of sixteen, Darwin spent two years as a medical student at the University of Edinburgh, where he observed at close quarters how different sectors of the local populace had evolved. Hutton would eventually be honoured as the 'founder of modern geology' and furthermore was responsible for millions of students being guaranteed marks as long as they remembered to write 'erosion' in their geography exams.

EDINBURGH NEW TOWN

Edinburgh may no longer be a capital city of an independent country but began to be transformed with the draining of the Nor Loch in the 1760s and the construction of the New Town, designed by James Craig, in the 1770s. The wide new streets of George and Queen Street being especially designed to enable thousands of tourists to take a nice picture of the Castle while aimlessly wandering as far from the bagpipe players as possible.

George Street was named after King George III,

Princes Street (which usurped Craig's vision of George Street as the city's main thoroughfare) was named for his son George (later King George IV) and Frederick Street after his son Frederick. Hanover Street was named after the Royal Family and Charlotte Square was named after Queen Charlotte. Luckily there were no royal corgis at the time as otherwise we would have had Benji Street and Shep Avenue as well.

The first stage of Craig's New Town was completed in 1800. Charlotte Square had been designed by Robert Adam (1728–92) from Kirkcaldy, who was considered Britain's greatest architect of the 18th century, renowned for leading the classical revival in British architecture. Adam turned his elegant hand to everything from stately homes and castles to public buildings and bridges, from Edinburgh University's Old College to Culzean Castle in Ayrshire to Pulteney Bridge in Bath.

Number 6 Charlotte Square was named Bute House after its former owner, the Marquis of Bute, transferred it to the National Trust in 1966. The National Trust, in turn, loaned the house to the government as the official residence of the Scottish Secretary of State and, since 1999, it has become the official residence of the Scottish First Minister.

Robert Adam's father, William, and his brothers, John and James, were also famous architects but there is little evidence of the Adams' family being creepy, kooky, mysterious or spooky, and ooky simply isn't a real word.

The next major building development in Edinburgh began on Calton Hill in 1822. An Acropolis was designed, probably to emulate the Parthenon in Athens, which was intended as Scotland's National Monument in memory of those who fought in the Napoleonic Wars. Sadly, funds soon ran out and what is now known as 'Edinburgh's (or Scotland's) disgrace' remains unfinished, which was probably just as well as Lord Elgin would no doubt taken most of it away anyway.

THE ENLIGHTENMENT

The latter half of the 18th century became know as the Scottish Enlightenment with some of the greatest figures in the world of the arts and science living in Scotland. Edinburgh was awash with thinkers, writers, scientists and architects who liked nothing more than discussing metaphysical philosophy while sipping a wee dram or two.

ADAM SMITH

Adam Smith (1723–90) from Kirkcaldy was a moral philosopher and economist who wrote the hugely influential treatise *An Inquiry Into The Nature And*

Causes Of The Wealth Of Nations. The work was published in 1776 and discussed the market economy and free trade. Smith's ideas became the template for capitalism and the free market economy that was still inspiring Conservative politicians 200 years later, although Smith's belief that the wealthy had a moral responsibility for the poor did tend to be forgotten.

DAVID HUME

David Hume (1711–76) from Edinburgh was a philosopher and historian, a major figure during Scotland's enlightened age of reason and science and one of the most influential men in Europe. His many works included *A Treatise of Human Nature* in which he championed reason, logic and skepticism and argued that truth had to be proved. These beliefs brought Hume, who was also known for being a *bon viveur* with a keen wit, into repeated conflict with the Church of Scotland, who called him an atheist and a heretic and said that he would burn in Hell if he did not change his views, to which Hume replied, 'Not bothered, Hell doesn't exist, anyone fancy a pint?' – but in a somewhat more philosophical manner.

JOHNSON AND BOSWELL

It was the legendary French philosopher Voltaire who

said, 'We look to Scotland for all our ideas of civilization.'

Which was slightly different from Doctor Samuel Johnson's, 'Oats. A grain which in England is given to horses, but in Scotland supports the people.'

To be fair to the renowned literary figure and lexicographer Doctor Johnson (1709–84), he knew more about Scotland than most as in 1773 he set off on an eighty-three-day tour of the country with his biographer James Boswell (1740–95). They started in Edinburgh and travelled through the Highlands before reaching the islands of Skye and Mull. Both Johnson and Boswell wrote best-selling books about their journeys, and in the process invented the celebrity travelogue that has become so popular – although the footage for the accompanying TV series *Long Way North* has been sadly lost.

The *Encyclopaedia Britannica*, the most famous encyclopaedia in the English language, was first published in Edinburgh in 1768 and by 1801 was up to twenty volumes. The Encyclopaedia continued to be published in Scotland until 1901, when financial difficulties and Scotland's shortage of doors for salesmen to knock on saw it being sold to a US publisher.

ROBERT BURNS

Even more famous and influential than Smith and Hume was a young poet from Alloway in Ayrshire by the name of Robert Burns (1759–96). He wrote poems and songs, mainly in Scots rather than English, and had his first collection published in 1786 called the Kilmarnock Edition that immediately became a national bestseller. In 1787 Burns spent time in Edinburgh and the rest of Scotland, where he was acknowledged as a major new literary talent. Burns' time in Edinburgh also allowed him to get away from the financial difficulties he was facing on his Ayrshire farm and, more pressingly, the disgruntled families of the women he had been having affairs with.

Burns wrote of the land, people, women and country that he knew and in such songs and poems as *Ae Fond Kiss, And Then We Sever*; *A Red, Red Rose*; *To A Mouse*; *Holy Willie's Prayer*; *A Man's A Man For A' That*, and the epic *Tam O' Shanter* (1791) he would expertly switch from love to satire to patriotism to humour and back again.

Burns returned to farming in 1788, finally getting around to marrying Jean Armour who had already given birth to four of his in total twelve children by four different women. In 1791 he became an exciseman in Dumfries. Burns liked a drink, was fond of the company of women and spoke his mind. He was only thirty-seven when he died in Dumfries, but became Scotland's favourite son and national bard, loved by all classes and Scots of differing political persuasions.

Many famous quotations come from Burns: 'The best laid schemes of mice and men', 'A gentleman and a scholar', 'Man's inhumanity to man', 'To see ourselves as others see us', 'Now's the day and now's the hour' . . . And in a somewhat different vein from his posthumously published collection of erotic verse *The Merry Muses of Caledonia* 'Nine inch will please a lady'.

NEW YEAR

The Burns poem *March to Bannockburn* with its opening line, 'Scots, wha hae wi Wallace bled,' was for a long time an unofficial Scottish national anthem and is still the party song of the Scottish National Party, but the bard's most famous work is unquestionably *Auld Lang Syne* which has become the theme tune to the celebration of New Year throughout the English speaking world, despite the vast majority not having the slightest idea what auld lang syne actually means.

New Year is traditionally the most popular annual celebration in Scotland, even compared to Christmas, with two public holidays set aside, on 1 January and 2 January, for some of the population to recover from the festivities and the remainder to contemplate whether the next twelve months will be as miserable as the last twelve.

The New Year festivities in Edinburgh have recently become some of the biggest in the world with thousands of visitors travelling to enjoy the entertainment, hospitality and Force 9 wind of a Scottish Hogmanay.

HAGGIS

Robert Burns' birthday on the 25 January became a national day to be celebrated by the copious consumption of haggis and lashings of turnips, washed down with whisky. Burns Suppers have become a regular feature not just in Scotland, but throughout the world, and are internationally a more popular celebration of all things Scottish than St Andrew's Day (30 November).

Thanks to the popularity of Burns and Burns Suppers, haggis has become the national dish of Scotland. Due to the scarcity these days of the endangered native Scottish wild haggis, most haggis recipes will include the traditional ingredients of chopped up sheep's heart, liver and lungs mixed with oatmeal, onion, salt, spices and suet and a sheep's stomach to cook them in.

Vegetarian haggis – ingredients here can include beans and lentils – has, in recent years, become a popular alternative to traditional haggis, usually not because the diner is vegetarian, but because the diner has just been told what traditional haggis is made from.

A Burns Supper will include a recitation of the Burns poem *Address To A Haggis* featuring the famous line, 'Great chieftain o' the puddin'-race' – although you will find this claim disputed by supporters of that other Scottish delicacy, the white pudding supper.

PORRIDGE

Scotland's other national dish is of course porridge, which is a very simple, but very filling mixture of oatmeal cooked in salted water. Scottish porridge oats have become popular internationally as a breakfast dish with the option, these days, to add sugar, milk or cream. The importance of porridge is clearly shown in the children's story *Goldilocks and the Three Bears*, in which it is not the breaking of the chair or the sleeping in the bed that infuriates the three bears, but it is the eating of the porridge that is just unforgivable.

Porridge became known as a dish that was given to prisoners throughout Britain, which in turn led to the TV comedy series *Porridge* (1974–77) in which Fulton Mackay played a distinctly Presbyterian prison officer who you could guarantee had his porridge with just salt.

It's Grim Up North

INDUSTRIAL REVOLUTION

The 19th century saw Scotland become an industrial country turning out cotton, coal, iron and steel. The Forth and Clyde Canal, completed in 1790, and the Caledonian Canal, completed in 1822, enabled goods and materials to be transported from one side of Scotland to the other. Scotland's industries required a large manual workforce and, therefore, many people moved from the country into the cities.

Glasgow, which had a population of only 31,700 in 1750 had grown to 147,000 in 1821, overtaking Edinburgh by some 9,000 in 1821 and reaching a staggering one million inhabitants in 1921, by far the biggest city in Scotland.

Rapidly growing cities built houses, hospitals, schools, civic buildings, sewers and city parks. The middle classes became more prosperous and cities became divided along class lines, with the working classes packed on top of each other in tenements where you were lucky to have head lice to call your own. By 1914 one third of all Scots lived in one of Glasgow, Edinburgh, Aberdeen or Dundee.

SCIENCE

Scots became pioneers of science and engineering. John Loudon MacAdam (1756–1836) from Ayr, for example, invented the Macadamised road surface – small stones bound together with gravel were laid over a base of large stones, then compacted and cambered – which, years later, when tar was added in became tar macadam (Tarmac). Macadam's work transformed British roads and the speed with which mail and goods could be moved around between Scotland and England.

Thomas Telford (1757–1834) from Westerkirk, Dumfries built roads, bridges and harbours throughout Britain, although he is best known for building the Caledonian Canal in Scotland, the Göta

Canal in Sweden and the Menai suspension bridge in Wales. The English midlands town of Telford and Telford College in Edinburgh are named after him.

William Murdoch (1754–1839) from Ayrshire invented gas lighting in 1792, Joseph Black (1728–99) discovered carbon dioxide – the chemistry buildings at both Edinburgh and Glasgow University are named after him. All these scientific greats were following the tradition of John Napier (1550–1617) of Edinburgh, after whom Napier University is named. Napier was the mathematician who discovered logarithms and the decimal point. So successful were the arithmetic techniques of Napier that calculators were banned for the next 400 years.

JAMES WATT

William Symington (1763–1831) built the first steamboat in the world in 1802. His invention had been inspired by one of Scotland's greatest ever inventors, James Watt (1736–1819) from Greenock.

Watt was an engineer who first invented a condensed steam engine in 1765 and then, in 1782, a double-action engine that used steam pressure – inventions that would be developed to power the Industrial Revolution of the 19th century. And Watt would have the international (SI) unit of power named after him (watt, kilowatt, megawatt, more powerful than you could ever imagine watt etc.) as well as Heriot Watt University in Edinburgh.

The story goes that Watt's interest in steam began as a young man when he observed the process of a kettle heating on a fire, although as with most kettles it took an interminable time for his ideas to come to the boil.

TOBACCO

The Act of Union between England and Scotland gave Scottish merchants access to the English colonies in America and the Caribbean and tobacco was the first commodity to bring major dividends. From the 1740s to the 1770s huge quantities of tobacco from Virginia and Maryland were imported to Britain and much of it was shipped to Glasgow and Greenock. Merchant families in the west, such as the Glassfords and the Buchanans, became very, very rich – they were known as the Tobacco Lords and many of them built huge properties in Glasgow. At one stage, tobacco comprised half of all Scotland's exports and one third of all Scotland's imports. Over the course of just a few decades the city had become established as a major international port and, in return, Glaswegians have shown their gratitude by happily contributing to the prosperity of the tobacco industry to this day.

As well as tobacco, Glasgow was ideally placed to supply goods to the Colonies. Even when the tobacco industry came to an end with the American War of Independence trade continued, and from the 1780s tobacco was replaced by cotton. And even Robert Burns nearly went to Jamaica in 1786 where he planned to work on a sugar plantation and become the original Mr Loverman.

Of course, the entire tobacco, cotton and sugar industries were completely dependent on the generations of slaves being forced to work on plantations. Scotland may not have been actively involved in the slave trade to the same extent as England, but many Scots were plantation owners in the West Indies. In view of the vast income that tobacco and cotton brought to Scotland, it could be said that the country's economic success at that time was down to slavery. Britain did not bring in the Abolition of the Slave Trade Act until 1833.

NEW LANARK

The most famous cotton mills in Scotland were at the village of New Lanark, founded by David Dale in 1785, on the River Clyde. Under Dale's son-in-law

Robert Owen ownership, New Lanark employed 2,500 people and became famous for pioneering social and welfare benefits for workers, health and education for their families and an early attempt at dress-down Fridays. The mills closed down in 1968, but the village was preserved as a tourist attraction and World Heritage Site.

IRISH

At the start of the 19th century, Catholics only made up one per cent of the Scottish population, mostly in the Hebrides. By the end of the century the Catholic population had risen to twelve per cent through significant immigration from Ireland, particularly after the Potato Famine. The Catholic Irish settled mainly in Glasgow and Dundee, where they would make up a quarter of the population, lived in the worst parts of the cities, took the poorest paid jobs and suffered discrimination and racism from the inhospitable Scots. Not that all Irish immigrants to Scotland were Catholic, twenty-five per cent came from the Protestant North of Ireland and worked mainly in better paid jobs on the Clyde and found it easier to settle into Scottish society. The Irish Protestants also brought from Ulster an increased interest and support in Orangeism to Scotland. With the setting up of

Orange Lodges and Orange marches they were less than kind to their fellow Irish immigrants.

Scotland's reluctance to accept Catholics into society would see the immigrants living in their own areas of cities (such as the Gorbals in Glasgow) forming their own football clubs (Celtic in Glasgow and Hibernian in Edinburgh) and setting up their own schools which were incorporated into the state system in 1918 whilst retaining their Catholic identity.

In 2001, Catholics made up sixteen per cent of the Scottish population, in 1969 Gordon Gray became the first Scottish cardinal for 400 years and in 1982 John Paul II became the first Pope to visit Scotland when more than 300,000 attended a Papal Mass in Glasgow, where he was given a Scottish football shirt and the congregation sang 'Will Ye No Come Back Again?' Unfortunately however, Kenny Dalglish had forgotten to sign the shirt and a disappointed John Paul never returned.

Therefore to recap: The Irish came to Scotland in the 6th century and were given the name Scots. The Scots then went to Ireland in the 16th century and settled in the North. The Irish then came to Scotland in the 19th century and settled in Glasgow and Dundee. And from the 18th century onwards Scots, Irish, Irish who used to be Scots and Scots who used to be Irish, all emigrated to America. Just imagine how confusing it would have become if the Welsh had got involved as well.

THE CLYDE

Glasgow was the fastest growing city in Europe in the 19th century as steel and shipbuilding industries grew along the Clyde. Such dramatic expansion saw the river polluted, contaminated water and open sewers leading to thousands of deaths in repeated cholera and typhoid epidemics with 10,000 alone dying in 1832. Although as fast as they died, there were thousands ready to take their place

The 1850s saw the introduction of clean water and sewers to be followed over the rest of the century by street lighting, a city transport system, Kelvingrove Park and the City Chambers which were opened in 1888. The Glasgow Subway was opened in 1896 serving 15 stations north and south of the Clyde and is the third oldest underground system in the world.

When Govan and Partick were incorporated into the city boundaries, Glasgow had increased its area as well as its population, which had gone from 150,000 to over 1 million within a hundred years. Glasgow called itself the Second City of the Empire, although everybody else called Glasgow the Birmingham of the North.

SHIPBUILDING

In 1812, Henry Bell built the steamboat *Comet,* which is widely considered to have inaugurated the first commercial passenger service, along the Clyde to Glasgow and Greenock.

The *Cutty Sark* was built at Dumbarton in 1869. She was given the name from the line in *Tam O' Shanter* by Robert Burns which described a cutty sark as a short shift, a ladies undergarment which was rather on the revealing side. The tea clippers were the last of the great sailing ships that sailed around the world before being replaced by steamships. The *Cutty Sark* became a museum ship in 1954 and a famous tourist attraction at Greenwich in London until she suffered serious fire damage in 2007. She is now being restored.

Glasgow's Clyde shipyards became the most important in the world. By 1900 they were launching more than 500,000 tonnes of ships a year, nearly twenty per cent of all shipbuilding in the world. Shipbuilding on the Clyde remained a major industry up until the 1950s with famous shipyards owned by Yarrow's, John Brown's and Harland & Wolff and the launching of great ships such as the *Lusitania* and the *Queen Mary*. The *QE2* was launched in 1967 and by then the industry was in steep decline due to international competition and the inconvenience of no war since 1945.

The remaining shipyards merged as the Upper Clyde Shipbuilders but went into receivership in 1971. When the government at first refused to support them, workers led by Jimmy Reid staged a work-in to show there was still a future for shipbuilding on the Clyde, a demonstration which gained huge public support and forced the government to put money into the business. Today, there are still working Clyde shipyards at Scotstoun and Govan, but the giant Finnieston Crane, which was built in 1932 and had become a symbol of Glasgow and the Clyde, has not been used since the 1990s.

The predecessor to the *QE2* was the *Queen Elizabeth*, named after the then queen and future Queen Mother (1900–2002), which was launched in 1938 as the world's largest passenger liner and was used during the war as a troopship. She was well built, broad and good in all weathers and interestingly the ship shared many of these characteristics.

RAILWAYS

Scotland was also at the forefront of the growth of railways. The first public line between Kilmarnock and Troon had been opened in 1812 but it was not until the 1840s that major expansion took place, by the end of the 19th century linking all of the mainland of Scotland. Glasgow became a major international producer of locomotives and the North British Locomotive Company exported its engines all over the world.

The first rail bridge to cross the Tay and Fife to Dundee was built in 1878, but collapsed in bad weather in 1879 with the loss of 75 lives. The second Tay Bridge was built in 1887 and still stands today. The builder of the second bridge was William Arroll (1839–1913) who would go on to construct the Forth Bridge and Tower Bridge in London. The Forth Bridge was completed in 1890 and was the longest bridge in the world when opened. It linked Edinburgh to Fife and is 2.5km (1.5 miles) long and is world-famous for its cantilever design and dramatic red colour, which led to the belief that there is a permanent team of maintenance workers on a never-ending exercise of painting the bridge. This is sadly not the case as sometimes B&Q are unfortunately out of stock.

The Forth Bridge featured in the 1935 film version of *The 39 Steps* based on the best-selling novel by

Scottish writer and politician John Buchan (1875–1940) from Perth. In the film directed by Alfred Hitchcock, the hero Richard Hannay escapes from a train on the middle of the Forth Bridge and hides behind a girder, although it is never explained how he then ends up in the next scene running from the police in the Perthshire Highlands.

The train that Hannay is travelling on is the famous *Flying Scotsman*, which was the name given to the service from London to Edinburgh that began in 1862. The Flying Scotsman was also the name given to Eric Liddell (1902–45), the famous athlete and missionary who won an Olympic Gold medal for the 400 metres at Paris in 1924 and whose story was told in the 1981 Oscar-winning *Chariots of Fire*, that also featured the scene of the British Olympic team running very slowly along the sands of St Andrews.

The Glenfinnan Viaduct on the West Highland Line rivals the Forth Bridge for international iconic status. The picturesque location was already well known but became even more famous when it appeared in the film version of *Harry Potter and the Chamber of Secrets* when Harry and Ron crash a flying car after missing the *Hogwart's Express*. This dramatic incident would also have a knock-on effect for passengers on the late-running Fort William to Mallaig service.

BRIDGES

The Tay Bridge (the railway bridge that connects Dundee and Fife) is the longest bridge in Scotland at more than 3.1km. The Forth Bridge between Edinburgh and Fife is the second longest at over 2.5km. The Tay and Forth Road Bridges are third and fourth. Fifth is the Kessock Bridge at 1km between Inverness and the Black Isle. The Skye Bridge that connects the island to Kyle in the mainland was opened in 1995 and is the seventh longest bridge at 570 metres. A controversial toll system was introduced for the bridge that made the Skye Bridge the most expensive road in Europe until the tolls were finally abolished in 2004.

The Tay Bridge Disaster was commemorated in a famous poem by William McGonagall (1825–1902), who was born in Edinburgh and moved to Dundee and became celebrated as the worst published poet in the English language. *The Tay Bridge Disaster* is his most famous work and features the lines:

'And the cry rang out all o'er the town,

Good Heavens! the Tay Bridge is blown down,' . . .

COAL INDUSTRY

Coal had been mined in Scotland since the 12th century, but expanded greatly in the 19th century as the Industrial Revolution required fuel. The work was hard and dangerous, but the industry expanded with coalfields and collieries throughout Fife, Lanarkshire and Midlothian and Ayrshire and many mining villages such as Cowdenbeath and Newtongrange. The coal mining industry began to go into decline after World War I, when 150,000 worked in the industry in Scotland, but was still one of Scotland's major industries when the Labour government nationalised the pits in 1947. The Scottish mining community celebrated, believing they had secured jobs for life and the state would look after them but, with continued redundancies and closures, by 1979 there were only 20,000 Scottish coal miners left in the industry and boys and men from mining villages would have to think of less subterranean locations for their employment prospects.

SHEEP

The Highlands were untouched by the Industrial Revolution, remaining rural and concentrating on traditional forms of farming. Farming in the Lowlands had been transformed by agricultural reforms and the new post-Culloden Highland landowners, no longer the traditional clan chieftains, but absentee lairds from Scotland and England, wanted more profit from their land. Sheep were to be the answer. Inexpensive, durable and requiring little maintenance, sheep could multi-task by providing meat, wool and little fluffy lambs. The Scottish Blackface was joined by the larger Cheviot, a white-faced sheep from the Borders. This breed proved so popular with landowners throughout Scotland that 1792 became known as the Year of the Sheep, probably not one of the most exciting years in Scottish history.

CLEARANCES

The only real drawback with sheep was that they required land to graze on. The solution therefore was to remove people and replace them with sheep. If the people would not be persuaded to leave quietly then forcible evictions took place. The first clearances in the Highlands and Islands took place in the early 19th century, although most tenants were moved to the coast to work in fishing and the kelp industry. The most notorious clearances took place in Sutherland between 1812 and 1819 when Elizabeth, Countess of Sutherland (1765–1839) and her factor Patrick Sellar forcibly moved up to 10,000 people out of their homes.

The second major stage of the Clearances took place after the potato crop failed in 1846. While not resulting in the catastrophe of the Irish potato famine, the process of depopulation was accelerated with thousands leaving the Highlands either for the cities of the Lowlands or overseas to America. Whether voluntarily or not up to two million Scots left in the 19th century to find new lives further afield. The Highlands became a sheep's world with only the occasional intrepid hill-walker disturbing the zen-like equilibrium of a flock of Cheviots.

CROFTING

The term croft meant a small agricultural landholding that was worked by tenants in the Highlands and Islands from the 18th century. The crofter rented his land from the landowner who was called the laird. Disputes between crofters and lairds intensified through the late 19th century culminating in The Crofters War in 1882 in Skye when landlords refused crofters' requests for more land to graze sheep and the crofters refused to leave their land or pay rent when the landlords refused. The police were called in but for once public opinion was on the side of the crofters and the government set up a commission to look into the whole issue of crofting and the rights of the crofters who had lived and worked on their land for generations. In 1886 the Crofters Act finally gave them security of tenure over their land, bringing some form of stability to the few remaining Highlanders, Islanders and Border Collies that were left.

GAELIC

The depopulation of the Highlands and Islands in the 19th century saw a major decline in the Gaelic language. Gaelic was a Celtic language that had flourished as the language of the Scots people from the 5th through to the 11th century, with Alba the Gaelic name for what we now call Scotland. Gaelic was however not the language of Lothian and it was English and its Scots derivation that became the language of the court, of parliament, of the law and of the Lowlands. Gaelic lost its hold over the North East of Scotland in the 13th century, but remained overwhelmingly the language of the Highlands and Hebrides until Culloden and beyond with up to half of Scotland's entire population either Gaelic speakers or able to speak both Gaelic and English.

After Culloden, the Gaelic language was first banned and then discriminated against for centuries. The 1872 Education Act which brought free education to all ignored the language altogether. By 1901 there were still 250,000 Gaelic speakers left in Scotland, but the 20th century saw continued depopulation, neglect and decline and by the 1970s there were less than 100,000, predominantly all in the Islands. The last thirty years have seen major attempts from central and local government to stem the decline with investment into education, street signs and broadcasting. However, by 2001 Gaelic speakers were down to 58,000 (one per cent) of the entire Scottish population and Gaelic television was reduced to the occasional hour of fiddle music or programmes on fish either broadcast at the same time as *Coronation Street* or in the early hours of the morning long after the entire potential audience had gone to bed.

FISH

From the 18th century up until World War One the herring industry was the main fishing industry in Scotland. Concentrated on the east coast, fishermen would sail out in open boats to catch them in huge numbers. With the advent of drift nets and engine power, the Scottish herring fleet became the biggest fishing fleet in Europe with nearly 2,000 boats following the shoals of herring from Shetland and Wick in the North to East Anglia in the South, with armies of up to 10,000 Scottish women at the harbour, gutting and packing up to two million barrels per season. The women would work in teams of three: two gutting and the other one packing the fish, and they would sing as they worked.

Herring were given the name the silver darlings, which means that Chancellor of the Exchequer Alistair Darling (1953–) is actually a big herring.

The herring industry went into decline after World War One and fishermen began to turn to fishing for cod and haddock using seine nets. The Scottish herring industry finally collapsed in the 1980s when stocks became exhausted. The only consolation being that nobody had to pretend anymore that they actually liked kippers.

In 1882 the first trawler left Aberdeen and soon a fleet of steam trawlers was sailing from Peterhead and Fraserburgh to transform the fishing industry in the North East and make cod and chips or haddock and chips a staple part of the diet of Scots everywhere. Fish and chips would traditionally be eaten with a dressing of salt and vinegar and accompanied by a bottle of Irn-Bru – except in more refined Edinburgh where they would have salt and sauce and a bottle of Blue Nun.

THE KIRK

Scotland remained a predominantly Presbyterian country with the Church of Scotland a dominant force in town and country life. The population may be expected to work long hours six days a week, fifty-two weeks of the year, but eternal damnation would be ensured if you so much as broke wind on the Sabbath.

In 1843 however a divide had appeared in the Church of Scotland between tall moderates and smaller fundamentalists who were sick and tired of going to the Kirk and not being able to see anything because of their tall colleagues standing in front of them. Eventually the smaller third of the Kirk broke away to form the Free Church or as they were affectionately known the 'Wee Frees'.

The Very Sharp Pen
Is Mightier Than The
Rusty Sword

WALTER SCOTT

Walter Scott (1771–1832) was born in Edinburgh and as a young man met Burns when the Bard visited the capital in 1787. Scott would go on to write poetry before publishing a series of bestselling historical novels from 1814 that included *Ivanhoe*, *Waverley* and *Rob Roy*. These novels sold throughout Europe and made Scott internationally famous while at the same time painting a picture of a romantic Highland Scotland, which for good or ill has remained to this day. When King George IV was persuaded to make the first royal visit to Scotland since Charles I in 1822 it was Scott who was given the job of organising the event and made Edinburgh a pageant of tartan and kilts. He also persuaded King George himself to wear a very short Royal Stuart kilt which most observers agreed the 20-stone plus monarch did not really have either the figure or the knees to get away with. The imposing 61m high Scott Monument in the centre of Edinburgh is named after the author and you can get to the top by walking up a narrow spiral staircase, at the end of which you will be rewarded with breathtaking views of the railway station and nearby shopping centre.

ART AND MUSIC

Many of the famous personalities who lived in Edinburgh during the Enlightenment had their portraits painted by Henry Raeburn (1756–1823). His most famous and popular painting is not technically a portrait but that of the Reverend Robert Walker skating on Duddingston Loch (unsurprisingly entitled *The Reverend Walker Skating on Duddingston Loch*) just before the minister falls through a crack in the ice.

The Skating Minister is to be found at the National Gallery of Scotland which was opened in Edinburgh in 1859. The most widely known painting by a Scottish artist however, is the *Singing Butler* by Jack Vettriano (1951–) from Kirkcaldy, which in poster and postcard form sells more than any other painting in Britain, despite or perhaps because of Vettriano's work being turned down by every single art gallery in Scotland.

In the summer of 1829 German composer Felix Mendelssohn (1809–47) came to Scotland for his summer holidays and travelled along the West coast. So inspired was he by his visit that he composed both the *Hebrides Overture* (1832) and the *Scottish Symphony* (1842). The *Hebrides Overture* is better known as *Fingal's Cave*, being inspired by the sea cave of the same name on the uninhabited island of Staffa. The Fingal in question was the Scottish name for the legendary hero known as Finn in Scandinavia and Fionn mac Cumhail (Finn MacCool) in Ireland. Fingal is often described as being a giant, and luckily his cave on Staffa is more than sixty feet high.

STEVENSON

Robert Louis Stevenson (1850–94) was born in Edinburgh and wrote some of the most famous books in world literature – *Treasure Island* (1883), *Kidnapped* (1886) and *Strange Case of Dr Jekyll and Mr Hyde* (1886), *Treasure Island* gave the world Captain Flint,

Long John Silver, Pieces of Eight, Black Dogs, Black Spots and the unhygienic fashion of keeping parrots on your shoulder. *Kidnapped* was an adventure story set in the Highlands after Culloden that featured both fictional and historical characters. *Kidnapped* was sympathetic to the Jacobites and less sympathetic to porridge-eating uncles who lived alone.

Stevenson was also part of a remarkable dynasty of engineers who built Scotland's lighthouses in the most inaccessible parts of the Scottish coast and have over the centuries saved thousands of lives. The first Lighthouse Stevenson was Robert Stevenson (1772–1850) who was Robert Louis's grandfather.

CONAN DOYLE

Arthur Conan Doyle (1859–1930) was also born in Edinburgh and found fame as the author of the world's best known and first opium-smoking, violin playing private detective, Sherlock Holmes. Holmes and Dr Watson were to feature in 60 stories and novels from 1887–1927 and numerous times on film and television. The most famous of the stories was *The Hound of the Baskervilles* (1901) that proved incredibly popular considering that the very title gave away whodunit.

J. M. BARRIE AND KENNETH GRAHAME

James Matthew Barrie better known as J. M. Barrie (1860–1937) was born in Kirriemuir and became famous for his children's play *Peter Pan* (first performed in 1904) that he later turned into a book. *Peter Pan* was made into a Walt Disney cartoon film in 1953 and has become a popular Christmas pantomime despite, or perhaps because of the role of Peter Pan always being played by a young woman in tights and knee-length boots. *Peter Pan* brought us the world of Neverland and the characters of Captain Hook, Tinkerbell, Tiger Lily, the Lost Boys and the Darling family, although no mention was made of their wee Scottish cousin Alistair. *Peter Pan* also saw the first recorded mention of the name Wendy as a girl's name and therefore it could be said that Barrie is partly responsible for Scottish Labour leader Wendy Alexander (1963–).

Another children's classic was written by Edinburgh-born Kenneth Grahame (1859–1932) who wrote *Wind in the Willows* (1908) and featured the four friends: Toad of Toad Hall, Ratty, Badger and Mole and their arch-enemies the Weasels (tarnishing the reputation of an entire species in the process).

MACKINTOSH

Charles Rennie Mackintosh (1868–1928) is Scotland's best know architect and designer. Born in Glasgow, Mackintosh's most famous work can be seen at the Glasgow School of Art, the Willow Tea Rooms in Glasgow and Hill House in Helensburgh. Mackintosh became famous for his unified schemes, innovative designs, roses, lots of white and chairs for people with very long backs. The modernity of Mackintosh's work did not bring him commissions and he left Scotland for Suffolk in 1914 with his artist wife Margaret MacDonald to concentrate on his painting. Since his death, Mackintosh's reputation has steadily grown in both Scotland and internationally and many people come to Glasgow to buy a souvenir Mackintosh mug or fridge magnet.

GREYFRIARS BOBBY

In 1912 a novel by Eleanor Atkinson was published called *Greyfriars Bobby* which was to be the basis of a Walt Disney film in 1961. *Greyfriars Bobby* was based on a real Skye Terrier (1856–72) who lived at Greyfriars Kirkyard in Edinburgh, spending the last fourteen years of his life loyally staying at the grave of his deceased owner. On his death, a statue of Bobby was built outside Greyfriars and thousands of tourists every year visit it. While London has Nelson's Column, Edinburgh has a scale model of a small dog.

MacDIARMID AND GRASSIC GIBBON

Writers such as poet Hugh MacDiarmid (1892–1978) and author of *Sunset Song* (1932), the first of the *Scots Quair* trilogy, Lewis Grassic Gibbon (1901–35), wrote of a Scotland struggling to come to terms with the loss of a generation killed in World War I, uneasy about the speed of social and economic change and anxious about the long build-up to the second

MacDiarmid was a member of the Communist Party of Great Britain and of the National Party of Scotland, but found it difficult to be in both parties at the same time. His most famous work was *A Drunk Man Looks at the Thistle* back in the days when people used to read poetry.

He also wrote the lines which inspired today's SNP MSPs to wear white roses when being sworn in at Holyrood:

'Only the little white rose of Scotland
That smells sharp and sweet – and breaks the heart.'

DISNEY

The 1953 feature film cartoon of J. M. Barrie's *Peter Pan* was but one of several classic films with a Scottish literary influence made by the great film-maker Walt Disney. The first full-length Disney live action film was Robert Louis Stevenson's *Treasure Island* in 1950 with Robert Newton shivering his timbers as Long John Silver. In 1953, *Rob Roy, the Highland Rogue* was loosely based on the novel *Rob Roy* by Walter Scott. Disney returned to Stevenson and to the Jacobites in 1960 with a version of *Kidnapped* with John Laurie, Private Frazer from *Dad's Army*, playing the miserly uncle Ebenezer. And in 1961 Disney came to Edinburgh to make an adaptation of *Greyfriars Bobby* based on the novel by Eleanor Atkinson. Just in case there was any confusion about what *Greyfriars Bobby* was about the film was given the title *Greyfriars Bobby: The True Story of a Dog*. The Skye Terrier who was playing Bobby did ask if the title could be *Loyal Dog* or even *Small But Cute Dog* but was told in no uncertain terms that it would just be *Dog*. Sadly Walt Disney died in 1967 and there were to be no more Scottish-based films, but he was to be affectionately remembered in the famous Glaswegian comment comparing his artistic merits to popular singer Bing Crosby, 'Bing sings but Walt disnae'.

The Plan Has Not Changed, The Plan Is To Conquer The World

EMIGRATION

At the beginning of the nineteenth century the British Empire covered a quarter of the planet's land area and Scots were at the forefront. Scots became merchants, bankers, teachers, doctors, politicians, clerks and missionaries, the latter being a position that Scots seemed particularly keen on.

Hamilton became the name of a town in Ontario, Canada and in the North Island of New Zealand. Perth became the capital of Western Australia with a population of more than one million. Dunedin, the Gaelic for Edinburgh, became a city in the South

Island of New Zealand and shared the same street names.

Aberdeen is a city in Washington State in the United States and the birthplace of Kurt Cobain as well as a harbour on Hong Kong Island. And Paisley Park, originally a municipal piece of ground in the West of Scotland, was to become the recording studio of Prince, formerly known as Squiggle.

SCOTTISH REGIMENTS

Scottish regiments and Scottish soldiers became an integral part of the British Army and the British Empire serving throughout Europe, North America, Asia and Africa and fighting in the Napoleonic Wars, the Crimea, India and South Africa bringing their own unique brand of bagpipes, kilts and extreme violence to assist the forces of civilisation. The oldest regiment was the Royal Scots (now part of the Royal Scots Borderers) that was first raised in 1633, with the Scots Guards following in 1642. The Royal Scots Greys (now part of the Royal Scots Dragoon Guards) were first formed in 1678. It was the Greys on their grey horses and shouting 'Scotland Forever' who led a famous charge in the Battle of Waterloo in 1815 against the French, but suffered horrendous and repeated heavy casualties and led an exasperated

Duke of Wellington to grumble about the historic inability of the Scots to follow straightforward and clear orders such as 'Just leave it, they're not worth it.'

The first Highland regiment raised had been the Black Watch in 1725, so named because of their dark tartan and became the 42nd Regiment (or the 'forty-twa'). The Black Watch were followed by other Highland regiments such as the Gordon Highlanders and Argyll Highlanders who both began in 1794 and the Sutherland Highlanders who in 1854 at the Battle of Balaclava in the Crimean War stood in a line two deep and repulsed more than 2,000 Russian cavalry and gained the name The Thin Red Line. The commander of the Thin Red Line was Colin Campbell (1792–1863) who later went on to lead the British response to the Indian mutiny of 1857. The Black Watch has been serving in Iraq since 2004 and their story was dramatised in the internationally acclaimed play *Black Watch* by Gregory Burke.

The Scottish regiments gained a fearsome reputation as fighters and in World War I the Germans gave them the nickname 'Ladies From Hell' which is remarkably polite considering the circumstances of trench warfare. After World War II many of the famous Scottish regiments began to be amalgamated until in 2006 the controversial decision was made to have only one Scottish regiment, The Royal Regiment of Scotland, with headquarters at Edinburgh Castle, which would consist of five regular battalions – Royal Scots Borderers, Royal Highland Fusiliers, The Black Watch, The Highlanders and the Argyll & Sutherland Highlanders and two territorial battalions.

CANADA

The first Scots moved to Canada in 1621 when a colony was set up in Nova Scotia, which was Latin for New Scotland. When the first major wave of emigration took place in the 1770s from the Highlands it was Nova Scotia and Prince Edward Island where the Scots settled, establishing Scottish Highland communities which retained their culture, traditions and Gaelic language. Even today there are 1,000 Gaelic speakers in the Cape Breton area of Nova Scotia. It was often said that the only difference between Nova Scotia and the Scottish Highlands was that a moose being let loose in your hoose would cause considerably more damage in Canada.

The 18th century saw a further 250,000 Scots emigrate to Canada, mostly to Ontario, but also in settlements right across to British Columbia on the

Pacific coast. It had been Alexander Mackenzie (1755–1820) from Stornoway who in 1793 had become the first European to cross North America from coast to coast, but unfortunately as he arrived on the Pacific coast on the Sabbath he felt obliged not to have a drink. Scots were at the forefront of the fur trade, cattle farming and politics with John A. MacDonald (1811–91) from Glasgow the first prime minister of Canada in 1867. The 20th century saw more than another 500,000 Scots emigrate to Canada and today fifteen per cent of all Canadians are proud to claim Scottish descent, although being Canadians they are not so much proud but more quietly satisfied.

BAGPIPES

At one time bagpipes were a popular instrument throughout Europe as all you required was a bag that could be made from animal skin and some pipes to put into said bag. However, from the Renaissance onwards Europe moved on to the more sophisticated melodies of Bach, Beethoven, Mozart and the Macarena, the pipes would only be found on the furthest edges of the continent, such as the Scottish Highlands. The creation of the Scottish regiments in the British army saw a second life for the bagpipes and they became the soundtrack throughout the

Empire where even the most implacable of foes would run screaming rather than face an advancing regiment of Highland pipers. The bagpipes attained huge popularity in 1972 when the Royal Scots Dragoon Guards got to Number 1 with their haunting version of *Amazing Grace*. Unfortunately all this goodwill and appreciation was then lost five years later when Paul McCartney released *Mull of Kintyre*.

SCOTS ABROAD

John Paul Jones (1747–92) became known as the founder of the American Navy and had the unique achievement in the American War of Independence of commanding an American raid on the Kirkcudbright coast where he was born. Thomas Cochrane (1775–1860) was an acclaimed Admiral who not only served in the British Navy, but also commanded the navies of Chile and Brazil in their Wars of Independence and was the inspiration for the fictional character Horatio Hornblower.

Lachlan McQuarrie (1762–1824) from the island of Ulva was Governor of New South Wales in Australia from 1810 to 1821, transforming Australia from being just a penal colony, giving rights to released convicts, making roads into the Australian interior, adopting the name Australia itself. Being a keen lover of seafood he was probably the first person to 'throw a shrimp on the barbie'.

John Muir (1838–1914) from Dunbar moved to America where he became famous as one of the first environmentalists whose writing and campaigning for the preservation of wildlife eventually resulted in the opening of Yosemite National Park in California in 1890.

Andrew Carnegie (1835–1919) left Fife at the age of 13 to make a vast fortune in the United Sates as the head of America's largest steel company. He then spent his latter years giving away £70 million (a huge amount of money back in 1900) of his vast fortune to charities, libraries and public initiatives in both Scotland and the US, including the building of the world famous Carnegie Hall in New York and the slightly less famous Carnegie Hall in Dunfermline. Carnegie also returned to Scotland in his retirement where he bought and lived at Skibo Castle in Sutherland, where in 2000 for reasons never fully explained Madonna married Guy Ritchie.

GEOGRAPHY

The largest cities in Scotland are Glasgow with a population of 580,000 and Edinburgh with a population of 450,000. However there are larger cities in the world with Scottish connections. In Canada Hamilton is a city in Ontario with a population of 700,000 compared to the town in Lanarkshire with a population of 50,000. And Perth in Western Australia has a population of 1.5 million compared to the old capital of Scotland with a population of 45,000.

In the United States of America, the two largest cities in Texas are Houston with 2.1 million and Dallas with 1.2 million. Both cities were named after American politicians who had Scottish ancestry, with their names coming from old Scottish villages. Houston is to be found in Renfrewshire with a population of 6,000 and Dallas is in Moray with a population of 200, but boasts several grassy knolls.

DAVID LIVINGSTONE

Mungo Park (1771–1806) was an early explorer to Africa, but it was David Livingstone (1813–73) from

Blantyre who found world-wide fame as a missionary, doctor, writer and explorer, travelling extensively through the African interior. Livingstone became the first European to see the largest sheet of falling water in the world Mosi-oa-Tunya, which he renamed Victoria Falls, and was in Africa without any contact for such a long period of time that an international expedition led by Henry Stanley was sent to find him. This led to the famous question when the two men finally met in 1871 of 'Dr Livingstone I presume?' and the less famous Scottish reply of 'Who wants to know?'

Livingstone was one of the first of a long line of Presbyterian Scottish missionaries and ministers who set up missions and churches throughout Southern and Central Africa. The country that was Nyasaland and now Malawi was run almost as a Scottish colony within the Empire and still has strong links with Scotland today.

Mary Slessor (1848–1915) from Aberdeen became famous for her determination as a lone woman to work and live with local people in Nigeria where she had to overcome hardship, disease and worst of all a complete absence of rowies (Aberdonian butteries).

QUEEN VICTORIA

The monarchy had abandoned Scotland with only one royal visit in 200 years until the succession of Queen

Victoria (1819–1901) in 1837. Victoria and her husband Prince Albert were frequent visitors to Scotland and bought the castle and estate of Balmoral in Aberdeenshire in 1852. Victoria and Albert wore tartan, danced to Scottish music, hosted ceilidhs, ate shortbread and in the process invented the modern Scottish tourist industry.

Victoria published her bestselling *Highland Journals* in 1868 and was soon followed to Scotland by the rest of the British establishment to enjoy the pastimes of hunting, fishing and shooting – although it was for a change deer, salmon and grouse rather than Highlanders. Although the gamekeepers and beaters were always a little apprehensive every 12th day in August, about how many of their number would end up as casualties in the general carnage of the Glorious Twelfth, the first day of the grouse-shooting season.

When her husband Prince Albert died in 1861, Victoria went into mourning and spent much of the next decade at Balmoral out of the public eye. Her faithful Highland servant John Brown (1826–83) was credited with having considerable influence over the queen and remained by her side until his death. Victoria was even given the nickname of 'Mrs Brown' (which was the title of the 1997 film starring Judi

Dench and Billy Connolly) as rumours circulated about the closeness of their relationship. Luckily Victoria was not made aware of any of these rumours, as she would not have been amused.

By the end of the 19th century with the sharp drop in wool prices, it was the turn of the sheep to be cleared from the Highlands to make way for huge estates of deer. The *Monarch Of The Glen* painting by Edwin Landseer became the representation of the Victorian view of the Highlands with its image of a magnificent stag. *The Monarch Of The Glen* TV series (2000–5), which was filmed in Badenoch and Strathspey, also gave a similarly idealised view of the Highlands and proved popular around the world with its image of a magnificent Dawn Steele.

BALMORAL

The Balmoral Castle and 24,000 acre estate, in what is now called Royal Deeside, has remained in the possession of the British Royal Family since 1852. Balmoral is the annual summer retreat of Elizabeth II (1926–), her family and the royal corgis. The Queen was in residence when Princess Diana died in 1997 and – as portrayed by Helen Mirren in the 2006 Oscar-winning film *The Queen* – was reluctant to leave Balmoral and return to London to face the national outpouring of grief as a surprisingly chipper Prince Philip had planned a Greek night that weekend.

INVENTORS

In 1872 free education would be made compulsory for every child in the country, no matter how rich or poor and no matter if the child wanted to go to school or not. Throughout the 19th century Scots continued to influence the world of science and the arts

James Clerk Maxwell (1831–79) from Edinburgh was one of the 19th century's most influential physicists. He discovered the links between electricity and magnetic fields and was hailed by Einstein as the founder of the modern scientific age, thus paving the way for his theory of relativity. Maxwell is also credited with explaining the nature of Saturn's rings and producing the world's first ever colour photograph in 1861 of a tartan ribbon, imported especially from China.

William Thomson, Lord Kelvin (1824–1907) invented the Kelvin scale of absolute temperature. James Dewar (1842–1923) invented the thermos flask and would have been appalled at the modern lightweight flask that smashes at the merest touch. William Ramsay (1852–1916) won the Nobel Prize for Chemistry in 1904 and discovered neon, xenon, helium and krypton. Ramsay therefore has the unique claim to not only being the first person in the world to be able to talk in a really funny high-pitched voice but also presumably being one of the first to know the real identity of Superman.

James Chalmers (1782–1853) took his slightly unhealthy obsession of wanting to lick Queen Victoria and turned it into a positive by inventing the adhesive postage stamp. Charles Macintosh (1766–1843) from Glasgow invented the waterproof coat that was made from rubberised cotton and raincoats throughout the world were given the name 'the mackintosh' in his honour. Kirkpatrick Macmillan (1812–78) from Dumfriesshire is believed in 1839 to be the first person in the world to build a bicycle that had pedals, although as he was fined in 1842 for knocking over a pedestrian in Glasgow, there was still much work to be done on the concept of brakes. And it was John Boyd Dunlop (1840–1921) from Ayrshire who developed the pneumatic tyre in 1888, founded the Dunlop Tyre company and made bicycles a worldwide craze, a universal form of transport and confirmed Scottish men's little talked about tendency for all things rubber.

ALEXANDER GRAHAM BELL

Alexander Graham Bell (1847–1922) was born in Edinburgh. He emigrated to North America where he experimented with sound technology. He patented an early form of the telephone in 1875 and in the following year in Philadelphia he is credited with the first public display of this new invention that would change the world. This involved a famous conversation between Bell and his assistant Thomas Easton:

Bell: 'Mr Watson, come here, I want see you.'

Reply: 'Mr Watson cannot come to the phone right now, please leave a message after the tone.'

It was additionally surprising that it was Bell who was considered to be the first person to use a telephone as Scottish men are considered to be the least likely people in the world to actually ever want to speak on the phone.

 INVENTIONS

So we have surmised that it was Scots who had invented logarithms, tarred roads, the free market economy, gas lighting, the steam engine, colour photography, the bicycle, a rubber tyre for the bicycle, the telephone and the waterproof coat. You would think that would be enough to be getting on with, but you would be wrong.

Neil Arnott invented a smokeless fireplace.

Alexander Bain from Caithness invented an electric clock and an early fax machine. David Brewster from Jedburgh invented the kaleidoscope. Dugald Clerk invented a two-stroke engine that could run on petrol. Robert Davidson invented the electric locomotive. Keith Elphinstone invented the car speedometer. James Nasmyth invented the steam hammer. Charles Tennant invented bleaching powder. James Lind found treatments for scurvy in the navy. Patrick Manson found the cause of malaria. Sandford Fleming from Kirkcaldy who moved to Canada devised the system of international time zones. William MacEwen was a pioneer in brain surgery. James Braid from Fife was a pioneer in hypnotism, or so he said. And Robert MacAlpine from Lanarkshire was a pioneer of concrete in construction and was given the nickname Concrete Bob. It has been suggested that MacAlpine was the inspiration for cartoon character Bob the Builder, but this is thought unlikely as he could only fix it if concrete was involved.

If The Drink Doesn't Kill You Then The British Army Will

TARTAN

Highlanders had worn tartan from early times, being simply the different coloured patterns in the woollen cloth that they wore and used around the house. After the defeat of the Jacobites at the battle of Culloden the British government was determined to ruthlessly crush what they saw as the Highland problem and one of their strictures was the banning of the wearing of tartan, although exceptions were made for the Black Watch and the other Highland regiments who had stayed loyal.

The ban on tartan was lifted in 1782 and sadly

after 36 years most of the kilts in the attic were looking a little shabby. Entrepreneurial weavers now saw the potential of a new market by linking particular tartans with particular clans. The clans had never bothered with having specific colours before, but in 1815 all clans had to register their particular tartan against their clan name. Some clans had no idea what their tartan might be and plumped for either one of the red ones or one of the blue ones, with the chieftains who were colour-blind ending up with the green tartans and the very, very drunk ending up with the yellow.

With a consistent list of official tartans in place, Scottish weavers and manufacturers could now market tartan throughout the world and produce kilts, shawls, cushion covers and shortbread tins. Tartan became an extremely popular design in the 19th century and was championed by Victoria and Albert, although in Scotland tartan was only ever worn by Highlanders, soldiers, the aristocracy, tourists and those that should have known better.

Tartan would become internationally fashionable from the 1970s onwards through the influence of punk designers such as Vivienne Westwood, although when New Romantics Spandau Ballet from London performed *To Cut a Long Story Short* on *Top of the Pops* in 1980 while wearing kilts, the Scottish Tartans Authority were appalled, although to be fair they were even more appalled when Spandau released the dreadful *Through the Barricades* several years later.

To complete your traditional Highland dress a tartan plaid would be worn over the shoulder and the obligatory knife carried for protection, either a dirk kept in your belt or a sgian dubh, Gaelic for black knife, a small dagger tucked into the sock. And of course no Highland outfit would be complete without the sporran, which is the Gaelic word for purse. The sporran would be made from leather or fur and as the kilt had no pockets would traditionally be where you kept your money, water, lip balm and photos of your children.

Tweed also became popular in the late 19th century and early 20th century as a woollen cloth for clothes, especially for outdoor wear and associated with the country set. Tweed gained its name from the River Tweed that runs through the Scottish Borders area where most tweed is manufactured, although the most famous tweed is Harris Tweed, which incongruously is made several hundred miles away in the Hebrides. Wearers have gained a reputation of being old-fashioned and conservative, with tweed today associated with cardigans, smoking a pipe and playing golf badly. This is of course completely unfair, as some tweed wearers are actually quite good at golf.

WHISKY

Scotland's national drink of distilled malted barley has been made from early times. The name whisky comes from the Gaelic *uisge beatha* and means 'water of life', which although not strictly true has been fervently believed by many Scotsmen, judging by the quantity that they can drink. To be classified as Scotch whisky, the spirit has also to be matured in oak casks in Scotland for a minimum of three years.

The whisky industry and the exporting of whisky began to develop in the 19th century, a process accelerated by the introduction of blended whiskies of malt and grain. Whisky became one of Scotland's biggest exports with huge markets around the world, especially in the USA, Japan, England, Europe and Asia worth up to £4 billion per year. Blended whiskies make up ninety per cent of the total Scotch whisky market with famous brands such as Famous Grouse (which is the most popular whisky in Scotland), Johnnie Walker, Whyte & Mackay, Bell's, Dewar's, Grant's and Chivas Regal.

Johnnie Walker is produced in Kilmarnock and an illustration of the original Johnnie Walker was used as the brand's logo, featuring Mr Walker striding in a purposeful manner – presumably in the general direction of the pub.

The remainder of the Scotch whisky industry mostly consists of traditional malts which are distilled in Speyside, which has the most distilleries in Scotland, as well as Inverness-shire, Perthshire, Campbeltown in Argyll, Islay, Arran, Jura and Orkney and includes such famous names as Glenfiddich, Glenlivet, Macallan, Glenmorangie, Highland Park, Talisker and Laphroaig.

Connoisseurs of whisky will spend lifetimes tasting and appreciating the large number of wonderful malts that are available, becoming expert in distinguishing the differences in water and peat used and perfecting the exact amount of water, if any, that should be added to each dram. The rest of the population can either not stand whisky or occasionally drink copious amounts of the stuff with ice, or God forbid lemonade, and deservedly suffer for days afterwards.

Popular whisky cocktails include a Rusty Nail which is whisky with drambuie and ice, a Whisky Mac which is whisky and ginger, a Rob Roy which is whisky, vermouth and angostura bitters and of course a hot toddy which is a teaspoon of sugar, a teaspoon of lemon juice, whisky and boiling water and is ideal for those feeling under the weather, over the weather and oblivious of weather in general.

A traditional way to drink whisky is in a two handled shallow drinking receptacle called a quaich. The word comes from the Gaelic for a cup or bowl and although a quaich is now mostly seen as a decorative gift, it is still used for its original purpose although with the drawback of requiring two steady hands rather than just one.

DRINK

Whisky is of course not the only drink that Scots partake of. In the early 19th century in Edinburgh and Glasgow there was a pub for every 150 people. Alcohol was also freely available in shops, so street drunkenness and binge drinking were exceedingly popular pastimes. In the more moralistic Victorian era, restrictions were put in place on the selling of drink. You could not get a drink on a Sunday for example, although determined imbibers got round this by drinking on boats that sailed down the Clyde which were not covered by the ban. From this the words 'steaming' and 'steamboats' came into the Scots vernacular as one of the 45 and counting different terms for being drunk.

Scotland's favourite alcoholic drink however

remains Tennent's Lager, first brewed in Glasgow in 1885 by the Tennent family who had been brewing since 1777 and now taking a market share of 600,000 pints a day, up to a quarter of all pints poured in Scotland. Part of the reason for the success of Tennent's Lager can be attributed to the pictures of the young women that featured on lager cans for 30 years up to 1991 and whose lovely smiling features would distract drinkers from intermittent feelings of gassiness.

Scotland's favourite non-alcoholic drink is Irn-Bru, first made in 1901 by A.G. Barr of Cumbernauld and is said to be more popular than Coca-Cola although as far as under-16s are concerned vodka and Coke still has the edge. Irn-Bru has become surprisingly popular in Russia where, much like Scotland, a considerable number of people are not only prepared to believe that Irn-Bru is the ideal cure for hangovers, but that a considerable number of people have hangovers in the first place. The actual formula for Irn-Bru still remains a closely guarded secret known to only a handful of people, although in a major security breach Barr's were forced to admit that girders may well be involved.

MOUNTAINS

Scotland is famous for its beautiful scenery and especially its magnificent mountains. Scotland boasts the highest mountains in the British Isles with Ben Nevis the highest of all at 4,408 feet. The word Ben is Gaelic for mountain or hill, which presumably means that an especially hilly hill would be called Benny Hill.

The 19th century saw mountaineering and hill-walking become a leisure activity. The term 'munro' was given to all mountains more than 3,000 feet high and was named after Hugh Munro who compiled in 1891 the original list and began the phenomenon of obsessive bearded men with flasks of tea walking up mountains in all weathers. There are now 284 peaks classified as being munros and munro-bagging is the term given to the practice whereby, when you reach the top and have your sandwich and chocolate bar, you should always put any rubbish in a little bag and take it back down with you.

WORLD WAR I

Not even the worst Scottish defeats of Flodden or Culloden or the countless other battles where Scotland came second out of two, came close to the number of casualties Scotland suffered in the Green

Fields of France and Belgium between 1914 and 1918.

Scots who joined up in August 1914 thought they would be home for Christmas, laden with fine French wine and cheese as victory presents. However, it was to be four years later at 11 a.m. on the 11 November 1918 before the killing finally stopped, at which time more than 100,000 Scots lay dead and nearly another 200,000 had been wounded. The Scottish regiments both Highland (still resplendent in their kilts) and Lowland fought with bravery and valour and sixty-seven Scots were recipients of the Victoria Cross. World War I had been given the name The Great War, but greatness had little to do with it.

The man in charge of Britain's World War I military campaign was Edinburgh-born Douglas Haig (1861–1928). Haig is a controversial figure in history who is blamed for being indifferent to the numbers of casualties and stubbornly following a policy of having his troops sit in muddy French trenches for years at an end interspersed with sporadic standing up and being shot at, thus resulting in the hundreds of thousands of deaths at battles such as the Somme and Passchendaele in 1916–17. Supporters of Haig on the other hand will point to the fact that, due to the strengths of the two forces, trench warfare was inevitable. Furthermore, after the War Haig became a devoted campaigner for the wounded and the widowed through the Earl Haig Poppy Fund and, in the final analysis, the British won the war, wearing down the Germans and thereby justifying his tactics and the number of men lost. This latter point might perhaps have more validity if the two countries did not end up going to war again twenty-one years later.

The major Scottish naval incident of World War I actually took place after the war had ended when in June 1919 the German fleet, which had been interned at Scapa Flow in Orkney since November 1918, scuttled fifty-one ships (including eleven battleships) in the greatest single loss of shipping the world had ever seen. Apparently this was in protest at the minimal fudge and Highland Park rations that the Germans were issued.

WOMEN

The Scottish Women's Suffrage Foundation had been started in 1906 by Elsie Inglis (1864–1917) who was also known for her work as a doctor and founder in 1901 of a maternity hospital in Edinburgh run by women. After being rejected by the Royal Medical Corps and Red Cross in World War I, she set up her own women-only ambulance units and military hospitals in mainland Europe.

Marie Stopes (1880–1958) was born in Edinburgh and became a campaigner for women's rights, family planning and birth control and was the founder of the international organisation of clinics that bear her name. At the time Stopes was a controversial and pioneering figure who was prepared to give explicit advice to women about how to have sex within marriage while avoiding becoming pregnant which climaxed in her manual on sex, *Married Love*, that was published in 1918. Her work was condemned by the established churches of the time who considered it obscene and there was much tutting at the Women's Guild back in Edinburgh.

With Scottish men fighting in the trenches in World War I, it was left to Scottish women to work in the munitions factories on Clydeside and keep the whole war effort going. Women had worked in the linen, cotton and jute industries for over a century, but there were now 200,000 women working in what was traditionally called man's work, producing the bullets, shells and bombs required to keep their menfolk busy. When landlords tried to exploit the huge increase in the munitions industry by increasing rents on housing around the factories, it was women led by Helen Crawfurd and Agnes Dollan who led the campaign against such blatant profiteering. The solidarity of the Rent Strikes of 1915 was so effective that it forced the British government to agree to freeze rent levels for the remainder of the war.

It was the vital importance of women in the war effort that was partly responsible for women finally getting the vote in 1918, although at first only women aged thirty or over were given the vote, as women under thirty were just too giggly.

In 1929 Jennie Lee (1904–88) became at the age of twenty-four a Labour MP for North Lanark and the youngest MP in parliament. Lee would later become in 1964 Minister for Arts and was given the task of setting up The Open University.

It was not until 1928 that women were finally given equal voting rights to men in Britain, although by this stage with the men back from the war and unemployment rising, a woman's place was once more back in the home, bringing up the children and making her man's tea for whenever he made it back from the pub.

War And A Jellie Peace

THE LABOUR PARTY

Throughout the 19th century there had been growing support for the improvement of conditions and rights for the workers in cities, towns, mines, yards, mills and factories that would result in the establishment and recognition of trade unions by the end of that century. In 1888, Keir Hardie (1856–1915) a former miner and journalist from Lanarkshire set up the Scottish Labour Party to represent the working class, followed by the Independent Labour Party in 1893 and then what we know now as the official Labour Party in 1900 which he led until 1908. Hardie became a Labour MP in London in 1892 and shocked parliament by wearing a cloth cap rather than a top hat in the chamber – just as well they never knew about his pet ferret.

Hardie believed in the rich paying higher income tax, women getting the vote, free pensions for the elderly, free education for all and the abolition of the House of Lords, so even today he would be considered ahead of his time. In 1906 Keir Hardie helped found the British Labour Party and was elected its first parliamentary Chairman. Scotland elected its first two Labour MPs in 1906 in Dundee and Glasgow.

However it was the 1906 Liberal government of Glasgow-born Henry Campbell-Bannerman (1836–1908), prime minister from 1905 to 1908, and his successor Asquith who implemented a radical agenda of economic and social change to tackle poverty, recognised the rights of workers and unions, set up public works to deal with unemployment, introduced state pensions and extended the vote to all men over the age of twenty-one – although women were still not to be trusted. However, it was also the Liberal government who had taken Britain into World War I and for that they were to suffer the consequences. In 1910 Scotland elected 58 Liberal MPs out of 72, but by 1924 this was down to 9, voted out by the ungrateful masses that they had given the vote to only six years previously.

RED CLYDESIDERS

If World War I was good for anything it was the munitions industry and the Clydeside heartlands of Glasgow, Clydebank and Greenock were at the forefront of the British war effort. The Clydeside had throughout the 19th century been at the head of the struggle to improve the rights of workers and the housing in which they lived. Through the combination of Clydeside's importance to the British economy, with steel and shipbuilding at their peak, and the growth of trade unions and political movements in the form of the Labour Party and the Independent Labour Party, Glasgow had become the most politically radicalised and socialist city in the country. Charismatic Clydesider leaders such as John Maclean (1879–1923) were openly anti-war and organised rallies against the conflict, but by January 1919 the war was over and Prime Minister Lloyd George had stated that Britain should be 'A Land Fit For Heroes' for the returning soldiers. In George Square in Glasgow, 90,000 attended a rally in support of a strike for a forty-hour working week and the Red Flag was raised at the centre of the rally.

The Glasgow rally was taking place just over a year since the 1917 Bolshevik Revolution in Russia and the British authorities reacted by sending troops and tanks from England into Glasgow to occupy the city. This government response was seen as being heavy-handed as most of the Clydesider leaders did not really consider the political potential of having nearly 100,000 people at their disposal, knowing full well that most of the marchers would want to get home for their tea.

At the 1922 general election twenty-nine Labour MPs were elected in Scotland, more than either the Liberals or Conservatives. Of those fifteen came from Glasgow and included Red Clydesiders James Maxton, John Wheatley and Emmanuel Shinwell. For Glasgow and the West of Scotland the moment for revolution may have been and gone, but the Labour movement had gained electoral power which they have maintained until the present, inspiring generations of politicians, activists and union leaders to fight the good fight, support the workers and at all times use a glottal stop wherever possible.

HOME RULE

British politics at the end of the 19th century and beginning of the 20th became preoccupied with the question of Irish Home Rule and Independence, eventually resulting in the creation of the Irish Free State in 1921. Almost as an afterthought the question of Scottish Home Rule was raised. To campaign for the better government of Scotland, and a parliament in Edinburgh, but not the breaking of the Union, a Scottish Home Rule Association was formed in 1886. Prime Minister Gladstone, who had reintroduced the position of Secretary of State for Scotland and created the Scottish Office in 1885 to look after Scottish affairs, also supported the idea of Scottish Home Rule, as did Keir Hardie and the Labour Party. Home Rule was debated several times in parliament, but with the House of Lords and the Conservatives against the proposal, no progress was forthcoming until the advent of the Liberal government and the curbing of the powers of the House of Lords' veto in 1911.

With the Liberals and Labour in favour, a Bill for Scottish Home Rule was put forward in 1913, was passed by the House of Commons and was seen at the time as a political inevitability. However, at the advent of World War I, civil war erupted in Ireland and afterwards the Labour Party, faced with the prospect of forming a UK government for the first time, began to lose interest in a Scottish parliament as compared to the bigger prize of running the whole British Empire.

An influential figure in the struggle for Irish Independence was James Connolly (1868–1916). Born in Edinburgh of Irish parents, he was a Scottish socialist before moving to Ireland where, in 1912, he was a founding member of the Irish Labour Party to campaign for an independent socialist Ireland. He was also commander of the Dublin Brigade at the Easter Rising of 1916. Connolly was so badly wounded in the Rising that when he was captured and the British decided to execute him, he had to be shot while sitting in a chair as he could not stand up. This action turned Connolly into an Irish martyr and Dublin's Connolly Railway Station is named after him.

SCOTTISH PRIME MINISTERS

The first Scottish Prime Minister of Great Britain was John Stuart, Earl of Bute who held the position in 1762–63 and was deemed so unpopular that no Scot was given the chance for nearly a century. The next was George Hamilton-Gordon, the Earl of Aberdeen (1784–1860) who held the office from 1852–55 but was blamed for taking Britain into the Crimean War, a conflict which nobody other than Florence Nightingale came out of very well.

There then followed a period where Scotland had considerable influence on British politics. William Gladstone (four times prime minister between 1868 and 1894) was MP for Midlothian and had a Scottish father. Arthur Balfour (Conservative prime minister 1902–05 and later famous for the Balfour Declaration of 1917 which saw Britain declare its support for a Jewish State in Palestine) was born in East Lothian. Henry Campbell-Bannerman (Liberal leader from 1899–1908 and prime minister from 1905–08) was born in Glasgow and was MP for Stirling. H. H. Asquith (Liberal prime minister from 1908–16) was an MP in Fife. Andrew Bonar Law (Conservative leader from 1911–23 and prime minister 1922–23) was brought up in Glasgow where he was an MP. Even future Prime Minster Winston Churchill (1874–1965) was MP for Dundee from 1908 to 1922 where he had the unique honour of becoming so unpopular that, in a city known for liking a drop of the hard stuff, he was defeated by a Prohibitionist. The idea of Britain having a Scottish prime minister is not so much unusual and constitutionally complicated, rather the normal state of affairs.

POLITICS

Since World War II, there have been two British prime ministers who represented Scottish seats: Alec Douglas-Home, MP for Perth & Kinross (1963–64) and Gordon Brown from Kirkcaldy (2007–until whenever the next election is). There have been two British chancellors of the exchequer, Gordon Brown (1997–2007) and Alistair Darling from Edinburgh South West (2007–); three foreign secretaries, Douglas-Home (1970–74), Malcolm Rifkind from Edinburgh Pentlands (1995–97) and Robin Cook from Livingston (1997–2001); two leaders of the Labour Party, John Smith from Monklands East (1992–94) and Gordon Brown (2007–) and four leaders of the Liberal Party, Jo Grimond from Orkney and Shetland (1956–67), David Steel from Tweeddale, Ettrick and Lauderdale (1976–88), Charles Kennedy from Ross, Skye and Inverness West (1999–2005) and Menzies Campbell from North East Fife (2005–07). An honourable mention should also go to Roy Jenkins who was Labour chancellor of the exchequer and founder of the Social Democratic Party, MP for Glasgow Hillhead from 1983–87 before he was defeated by 'Gorgeous' George Galloway, which presumably seemed a good idea at the time.

RAMSAY MacDONALD

Britain's first Labour prime minister was Ramsay MacDonald (1866–1937) from Lossiemouth. He was leader of the British Labour Party from 1911–14, when he resigned due to his opposition to World War I, and from 1922 to 1931 where he kept the party united against the potential rise of Communism to which MacDonald was strongly opposed. In 1924 MacDonald was briefly prime minister for nine months as head of a minority Labour government but was defeated by the Conservatives at the second 1924 General Election. However, MacDonald had proved moderate and respectable enough, with none of the Royal Family or House of Lords lined up against the wall, for the British electorate to give Labour a second chance in 1929. The second Labour government came to an end in 1931 when divided over what economic measures they should take to deal with the Depression, MacDonald resigned and set up a National government with Conservative support, which he led as prime minister to 1935. This decision by MacDonald would forever see him considered a traitor as far as Labour was concerned, even though it was under his leadership that Labour replaced the Liberals as one of Britain's two major political parties.

The question of Scottish home rule had been

forgotten at Westminster and the Scottish National Party was formed in 1934, but membership was small and public support smaller still as the country was divided between voting Labour and voting Conservative, with the Liberals down to only three MPs in Scotland by 1935.

ALEXANDER FLEMING

Alexander Fleming (1881–1955) was a doctor from Ayrshire who became a bacteriologist and lecturer in London. Fleming had been researching antibodies for years, but it was his unhygienic habit of never washing his dishes that was to result in his discovery in 1928 of a mould on his favourite coffee mug where bacteria did not grow. This would be identified as penicillin which further research would lead in the 1940s to mass production as a drug that could treat amongst others pneumonia, scarlet fever, meningitis and gonorrhea, thereby resulting in the saving of hundreds of millions of lives and making sleeping around a much less hazardous affair. Fleming would be awarded the Nobel Prize for Medicine in 1945.

Other influential Scottish physicians include James Young Simpson (1811–70) from Bathgate who was a pioneer in using anaesthetics to ease childbirth, following his discovery of chloroform it became the pain relief of choice when Queen Victoria used it during the birth of her last two children. Doctor and pharmacologist James Black (1924–) won a Nobel Prize for Medicine for his work in developing treatments for heart problems and his invention of the drug Propranolol (the world's first beta-blocker); and TV's country GPs John Finlay and Angus Cameron kept the good folk of Tannochbrae in good health in *Doctor Finlay's Casebook* from 1962 until 1971, with faithful housekeeper Janet ensuring the rubbing of ointment never became too enthusiastic.

JOHN LOGIE BAIRD

John Logie Baird (1888–1946) came from Helensburgh and was an engineer who, in 1926, became the first person to demonstrate a new-fangled moving picture invention called television and in 1928 was the first to demonstrate colour TV and to transmit pictures across the Atlantic. Baird also researched stereo sound and radio-waves and his television system was used by the BBC from 1929–37, before being replaced by a rival electronic system. At this time TV viewers were limited to several hundred in the immediate London area, much like the audiences for many BBC3 and BBC4 TV programmes today.

John Reith (1889–1971) from Stonehaven was the

founder and first director-general of the BBC from 1922 until 1938 and whose influence on public service broadcasting remained in place for decades. Reith was known for his high-minded, serious and moral views and would have been unlikely to have ever commissioned *Dick and Dom In da Bungalow*.

DEPRESSION

The 1920s and '30s brought to Scotland huge social changes in the form of the vote for women, cleaner water, electricity, gas, motor cars, buses, the telephone, the gramophone, the wireless and Laurel and Hardy. The 1924 Housing Act brought much-needed investment in more council housing for towns and cities. Unfortunately much of this housing remained traditional tenement one- and two-rooms, no matter how many dozen children the average family might have, and outdoor toilets remained the norm with one toilet per tenement and not an air-freshener in sight. It was no wonder that going to the cinema became so popular, where even Charlie Chaplin seemed hilarious compared to powdering your nose on a freezing February night.

Disease, poverty and overcrowding remained rife in Scotland's cities and economically Scotland continued to concentrate on the heavy industries of coal, steel and shipbuilding, but when the 1930s brought the Depression, mass unemployment hit Scotland with as many as thirty per cent of the working population unemployed in 1932.

Going to the cinema became one of Scotland's favourite pastimes in the 1930s with Glasgow alone having over 100 cinemas, more than anywhere else in the world outside the USA. In 1938, some of the gloom of the Depression was lifted by the Empire Exhibition that was hosted at Bellahouston Park in Glasgow and which saw twelve million people visit the many especially built sites displaying the best of Britain and her Empire. Sadly a year later, Glasgow and the rest of the British Empire was once more at war.

WORLD WAR II

World War II of 1939–45 saw Britain united across the country and across the classes to fight against Germany, Italy and Japan. Scottish soldiers and regiments fought in Europe, North Africa and the Far East.

Fewer Scots – 36,000 – died in World War II than in the carnage of World War I, but due to the Blitz and German air raids Scottish civilians were substantially more at risk. Glasgow, Edinburgh,

Aberdeen and Greenock were all bombed and suffered casualties from Luftwaffe bombing raids in which 6,000 Scots died.

The worst area affected was Clydebank which suffered two terrible evenings of bombing from 500 German planes in March 1941. All told 1,200 people were killed and a further 110 wounded, with 35,000 residents made homeless. So complete was the destruction that only seven houses in the whole of the town were left unscathed.

In World War II, Scotland's strategic position was vital to the battle for the North Atlantic with large naval bases in Rosyth, Invergordon and Gairloch, however it was at Scapa Flow that HMS *Royal Oak* was sunk by a German U-Boat in 1939 with more than 800 lost. It was further north in Shetland the same year that an unsuccessful German bombing raid resulted in the loss of one unfortunate rabbit which inspired the popular British wartime song by Flanagan and Allen of *Run, Rabbit, Run*.

The merchant navy criss-crossed the Atlantic in convoys and from 1942 the Arctic convoys began departing from Loch Ewe to the Soviet Union. Shetland's proximity to German-occupied Norway also saw secret sailings across the North Sea to assist the Norwegian Resistance under the name: the

Shetland Bus. And the Clyde continued to turn out warships.

One of the strangest events of World War II took place at a farm near Eaglesham in Lanarkshire on 10 May 1941 when Deputy Führer Rudolf Hess flew a Messerschmitt single-handed from Germany to Scotland, where he bailed out, breaking his ankle in the process, and was arrested by a man from the Home Guard who took him to his house for tea while he waited for the authorities to come. Hess had asked to be taken to see the Duke of Hamilton, who happened to live nearby, but was arrested and held prisoner until the end of the war when he was put on trail at Nuremburg and imprisoned at Spandau until his death in 1987. Great mystery still surrounds the real reasons why Hess came to Scotland. Was he on a mission from Hitler to end the war? Was he on a mission of his own? Why did nobody attempt to shoot his plane down? Was it really Hess? And why of all the places choose Lanarkshire?

RADAR

Arguably the most influential Scot in World War II was Robert Watson-Watt (1892–1973) from Brechin whose development of radar proved vital in the defeat of Germany. Watson-Watt had spent decades working on the subject before gaining a patent in 1935 and setting up air defence stations that could successfully use the new technology. By the Battle of Britain in 1940, the use of radar was to prove crucial in defeating the Luftwaffe and subsequently halt the Blitz in 1941. Without radar Britain would have been defeated.

LABOUR GOVERNMENT

In July 1945, two months after the end of war in Europe, Britain elected a new Labour government under Prime Minister Clement Attlee. They introduced the Welfare State, the National Health Service, nationalised the coal and steel industries and approved the first of Scotland's new towns – East Kilbride – followed by Glenrothes, Irvine, Livingston and finally Cumbernauld who would have as its slogan the phrase 'What's it called?', in acknowledgement of how memorable a place it was.

The Labour government were defeated by the Conservatives in 1951 who remained in power for the next thirteen years. In Scotland the Conservatives received more than fifty per cent support from the electorate in 1955. The Labour Party returned to power in 1964 and regained their position as the most popular party in Scotland. More than ninety per cent of Scots voted either Conservative or Labour, with the working class voting Labour, the middle class voting Conservative and the electorate of Orkney and Shetland voting Liberal under the mistaken belief that Lloyd George was still leading the country.

QUEEN ELIZABETH

Support for home rule had not gone away and in 1949 almost two million Scots signed a petition calling for its introduction, although support for the SNP remained negligible. On Christmas Day 1950 four Scottish students broke into Westminster Abbey and removed the Stone of Destiny. They had in their possession the most symbolic and important relic in Scottish nationhood, and immediately dropped it, with the stone breaking in two.

The students took both parts of the stone back to Scotland, 650 years after Edward had taken the stone to England, in, as it had been prophesied, a chariot that roared and raced like the wind, or to be more accurate a Ford Anglia.

The stone was buried, put back together with superglue and returned to the authorities in Arbroath Abbey in April 1951 and immediately taken back to London where it was used two years later for the coronation of Queen Elizabeth (1926–) in 1953.

Some Scots took exception to Elizabeth taking

the title of Elizabeth II of both England and Scotland when the first Elizabeth had only ever been queen of England. There had also been some complaints in 1947 when Elizabeth's husband Philip was given the title Duke of Edinburgh despite the Greek prince having no family connection with Scotland. However, the vast majority of Scots supported the monarchy no matter what titles they gave themselves and were only concerned about whether Philip would be able to get decent kebabs when he came to visit.

ROYALTY

As well as Prince Philip being the Duke of Edinburgh, Prince Charles holds the following titles in Scotland: Duke of Rothesay, Earl of Carrick, Baron Renfrew, Lord of the Isles and Great Steward of Scotland. Prince Andrew is the Earl of Inverness and Captain of the Royal and Ancient Golf Club of St Andrews. Princess Anne is the Patron of the Scottish Rugby Union and had her second wedding in Crathie Kirk near Balmoral. Prince William graduated from the University of St Andrews and Prince Edward went to Gordonstoun School in Moray (as did his father and brothers) where he was head boy. The queen on the other hand is just happy being the queen.

ST KILDA

The Labour government introduced hydro-electric schemes into the Highlands and Islands, bringing electricity to these areas for the first time and attempted to stop continuing depopulation. This was unfortunately too late for the remote islands of St Kilda, forty miles west of Harris. St Kilda was known as the Island On The Edge Of The World, although in fact St Kilda was the name given to the island archipelago and Hirta was the name of the main island. In 1930 after thousands of years of inhabitation the remaining thirty-six inhabitants asked to be evacuated rather than face another winter and left the island to the native Soay sheep who after two days of respectful rumination moved into the abandoned houses. St Kilda is also the name of the seaside resort of Melbourne and the name of an Australian Rules Football team from Melbourne who have come last more than any other team in their league.

All Fun And Games
And Then The Bottle
Crashed

GOLF

It was back in 1457 that James II banned the game
of golf for distracting people from archery practice
and for dangerous driving off the fourth tee. It is
believed that the sport originated in Scotland and
there is something inherently Scottish about men
going out on cold, wet days to hit a small ball with a
long stick for hours on end with no hope of
satisfaction at the end.

Golf was played throughout Scotland and by all
classes – Mary Queen of Scots was known to play and
would often take on John Knox in a nine-hole round

of matchplay with the religious faith of the country going to the winner; apparently both of them were known to cheat. In 1744 the first ever golf club was formed at Muirfield in East Lothian, to be followed by the home of world golf, St Andrews in 1754 where in 1897 the rules of golf were formalised. The course at St Andrews was given the title 'Royal and Ancient' in 1834, although as far as we know the Queen Mother never played there.

The first Open championship was held at Prestwick in Ayrshire in 1860 and the sport's popularity spread throughout Britain and beyond. Golf became a major sport in America and top American golfers Jack Nicklaus and Arnold Palmer revitalised golf in Scotland by entering and winning the Open in the 1960s and reestablishing the Claret Jug trophy as the most prestigious in world golf.

Five Scottish courses are currently venues for the Open – St Andrews, Muirfield, Carnoustie, Troon and Turnberry with more than 200,000 spectators attending – and these and many other top courses have made golf a major Scottish tourist attraction, popular with amateur golfers throughout the world who want to play at the home of golf and have the self-confidence to wear sky blue and canary yellow combinations in public.

FOOTBALL

Scotland can lay claim to being the home of modern football as in 1872 the first ever association football, or soccer or 'fitba' international in the world took place in Glasgow between Scotland and England. The entire Scotland team came from the Queen's Park club in Glasgow and the game ended 0–0 with both teams packing the midfield and playing for penalties – which unfortunately had yet to be invented for another hundred years.

The Scotland v England international became an annual event that would attract crowds of 100,000 at Wembley in London and even more at Hampden Park in Glasgow which was built in 1903 and was until 1950 the biggest football stadium in the world with attendance of up to 150,000. Scotland's most famous victory was in 1928 when, with a team including Hughie Gallacher and Alex James, Scotland defeated England 5–1 and were given the nickname the Wembley Wizards. There is circumstantial evidence that some of the huge crowds that attended these internationals might even have been sober.

Scotland's greatest post-war footballers are recognised as being Denis Law (1940–) who played for both Manchester City and United, and Kenny

Dalglish (1951–) who played for and managed both Celtic and Liverpool, although other world famous Scottish players included Dave Mackay, Jim Baxter, Jimmy Johnstone, Billy Bremner and Graeme Souness – who for many years sported the best moustache in world football.

1967 became the greatest year in Scottish football history with the national team defeating, and some say humiliating, the then world champions England at Wembley, and Celtic becoming the first British team to win the European Cup by defeating Inter of Milan 2–1 in Lisbon. The Celtic manager was Jock Stein (1922–85) who along with Matt Busby (1909–94) of Manchester United and Bill Shankly (1913–81) of Liverpool formed a triumvirate of Scots who built their clubs into some of the most famous in world football and established the blueprint of straight-talking, authoritarian, ruthless, successful Scottish-born managers who did not need a hair-dryer for hairdressing purposes.

RANGERS AND CELTIC

Football became the most popular spectator sport in Scotland with clubs being formed from the late 19th century onwards throughout Central Scotland, Dundee and Fife, as well as in Aberdeen and Ayrshire and huge crowds attending matches. The two most successful clubs in Scotland were Glasgow rivals Celtic (who play at Parkhead) and Rangers (who play at Ibrox).

Rangers came from a Protestant Unionist tradition and Celtic came from a Catholic Irish background. Between them they have won more than 90 of 110 Scottish League championships and have a rivalry that can be either seen as one of the most intense in world football or an excuse for the sectarianism and bigotry that has tarnished Glasgow and the West of Scotland for the past hundred years. The two teams have been given the name the Old Firm in recognition of their dominance of Scottish football and their success at turning religious intolerance into a highly lucrative business model.

SPORT

Scotland is world renowned for motor sport with world champions in motor racing and rallying. Two of Formula 1's greatest ever drivers were Jackie Stewart (1939–) from Dunbartonshire, three times world champion, and Jim Clark (1936–68) from Fife who was twice world champion before being killed racing in 1968.

The first ever rugby international in the world was

played at Raeburn Place in Edinburgh in 1871 when Scotland defeated England and since 1879 the countries have played each other for the Calcutta Cup. Rugby became particularly popular in Edinburgh and the Borders region and Murrayfield Stadium was opened in Edinburgh in 1925 – Scotland celebrated by winning the Grand Slam that year.

Famous Scottish rugby players include Andy Irvine, Gavin Hastings and commentator Bill McLaren from Hawick who became known as the Voice of Rugby and for his catchphrase 'They'll be dancing in the streets', which would later become a hit for Martha Reeves and The Vandellas.

The winter game of curling originated in Scotland and was taken by Scottish emigrants to Alpine Europe and North America where it became very popular in Canada, and curling became an official Winter Olympic sport, with a Scottish women's team winning gold in 2002 in Salt Lake City. Curling is believed to have originated in Scotland around the 16th century, although it is unclear when, or for that matter if, aimless throwing of stones on ice became an actual sport.

The Commonwealth Games will be hosted by Glasgow in 2014. Held twice before in Scotland, Edinburgh hosted an extremely successful games in

1970 but a return in 1986 proved less so when the capital was hit by poor weather, a boycott by the African nations and underfunding. The infamous businessman the late Robert Maxwell came to the financial rescue, and the unforgettable scene of the large-boned tycoon running onto the track to try and restore a flag on its pole is one of the earliest examples of what was later to become known as the Bouncing Czech.

CINEMA

Sean Connery (1930–) became the world's most famous Scotsman when he starred for the first time as James Bond in 1962. Connery would appear as 007 a further six times, but it is his first appearances in *Dr No*, *From Russia with Love* and *Goldfinger* that are still remembered today as the best of all the Bond films. Connery would later appear in many hit movies over the decades that included *The Name of the Rose* (1986), *The Untouchables* (1987) and *The Hunt for Red October* (1990). His star quality, charisma and longevity were recognised by both his peers in the film world and the general public: Hollywood awarded him the Best Supporting Actor Oscar for *The Untouchables* and the cinema-going public adored his portrayals from Irish cop, Spanish knight and Lithuanian navy captain to English king even if they did all appear to have the same Edinburgh accent.

Deborah Kerr (1921–2007) from Helensburgh became a Hollywood leading lady and starred in *Black Narcissus* and *The King and I*. Kerr also appeared in one of the most iconic scenes in cinematic history when in *From Here to Eternity* (1953) she and Burt Lancaster find themselves misjudging the tide somewhat on a deserted Hawaiian beach.

Bill Forsyth (1946–) achieved fame as the writer and director of two of Scotland's most famous films. *Gregory's Girl* (1981) not only achieved the remarkable goal of successfully combining romance, comedy and football but, even more astonishingly, managed to make Cumbernauld look relatively attractive. *Local Hero* (1983), Forsyth's comedy hit set in the Scottish Highlands also made famous a red telephone box in the North East fishing village of Pennan. Visitors from all over the world go to Pennan to see the famous telephone box and contemplate what life was like before mobile phones.

Local Hero was inspired partly by *Whisky Galore!* (1949), a comedy filmed on the island of Barra that told how a small Hebridean island took advantage of a ship sinking with its cargo of 50,000 cases of whisky. Ealing Studios' 1949 classic was adapted from

Compton Mackenzie's novel based on the true story of the foundering of the SS *Politician* off the Isle of Eriskay in 1941. The ship's cargo included some 25,000 cases of whisky to which the islanders had been helping themselves until, rather than let one more bottle of whisky go duty unpaid, the infuriated local customs officer had the ship's hull blown up.

The Prime of Miss Jean Brodie (1969) won an Oscar for Maggie Smith who played the title role in this film adaptation of the novella by Muriel Spark (1918–2006). Set in 1930s Edinburgh, Jean Brodie is a teacher at a girls' school and she called her pupils the 'crème de la crème', except when they set light to the science lab after which she called them crème brûlée.

Trainspotting (1996) was the film of the best-selling novel by Irvine Welsh (1958–) and starred Ewan McGregor (nephew of Denis Lawson who had starred in *Local Hero*). The novel detailed the drugs, sex, violence and high levels of swearing that accompanied the lives of young men from Leith and the parts of Edinburgh that tourists only encountered if lost, unlucky or with serious habits. The film was less explicit and extreme than the novel although there was still more than enough heroin and defecation to offend any unsuspecting viewers whose last Edinburgh-based film had been *Greyfriars Bobby*.

TOURISM

Tourism became an increasingly important part of the Scottish economy as higher standards of living, motorcars and air travel made visiting Scotland a more attractive and affordable prospect to people from Britain, Europe and North America. Descendants of Scots who had emigrated to the New World now had the opportunity to return to their roots. Many of these visitors were directly related to families who had been forced out during the clearances, which must have made dining out on roast Scottish lamb somewhat ironic.

In 1954 the Lerner and Loewe Broadway musical *Brigadoon* was turned into a popular Hollywood musical starring Gene Kelly and Cyd Charisse with Scotland portrayed as a country of castles, lochs, tartan, kilts, bagpipes, whisky and Highland Flings – and if that was what visitors were expecting then that was what the Scottish tourist industry would give them. The centre of Scottish tourism was Edinburgh with its castle, palace and festival. Other popular attractions for tourists included Stirling and Perthshire, playing golf at St Andrews and Troon, trying to spot the monster at Loch Ness, visiting the beautiful Highlands and Islands and keeping as far away from Glasgow as possible

THE FESTIVAL

The Edinburgh International Festival began in 1947 and the Edinburgh Festival Fringe (anything to do with the arts not already in the official Festival), which also started in 1947 but as a kind of splinter group, was named the following year. The Festival and the Fringe have since been joined by a film festival, television festival, book festival, jazz festival and the Didn't That Comedian Do Exactly The Same Act Last Year Festival. Together, these various festivals have made Edinburgh host to the largest cultural event in the world, with more than two million tickets sold every year and for four weeks every August turn Scotland's capital into a little enclave of London's West End.

The festival's most popular event is the Edinburgh Military Tattoo; every year, more than 200,000 spectators, plus millions more TV viewers, watch the massed pipes and drums, among others, perform all their greatest hits, six nights a week, on the castle esplanade.

One of the most influential shows staged in Edinburgh was *Beyond the Fringe* in 1960 written by and starring Peter Cook, Dudley Moore, Alan Bennett and Jonathan Miller, which is credited for launching the sixties boom in British satire. Curiously, *Beyond the Fringe* was in the International Festival and not in the Fringe at all.

It is often claimed that this glorious celebration of the arts is wasted on Edinburgh residents as they spurn the cultural opportunities that the Festival brings. This is of course a complete fallacy, as thousands of locals happily enjoy the free fireworks displays.

DUNDEE

Scotland's fourth largest city, Dundee became famous as the city of the three Js – jute, jam and journalism. The jute industry was so big in Dundee that at the beginning of the 20th century the majority of Dundee's workers were employed in the jute mills. The Keiller family from Dundee started the first ever marmalade factory in 1797. They became world famous for their orange marmalade which has become a breakfast staple on toast, or if you are Paddington Bear in sandwiches. And D. C. Thomson (1861–1954) set up business in 1905 and published, among other titles, comics – *The Beano* and *The Dandy* – and the *Sunday Post* newspaper which had at its peak in the

1970s a circulation of 1.5 million or one copy for every household in Scotland, although there would be trouble if Dad did not get to read it first.

Generations of children and adults throughout Britain have laughed at favourite D. C. Thomson characters such as Dennis the Menace and Gnasher and Desperate Dan. *Sunday Post* comic strip characters Oor Wullie (1937–) and The Broons (1936–) have become Scottish institutions and remain hugely successful. The Broons family consisted of Grandpaw Broon, Maw and Paw Broon, and their children Hen, Joe, Daphne, Maggie, Horace, the twins and the Bairn, although these days concerns would no doubt be raised about a family of eleven living in a small flat with three of the children apparently not even having a name.

NORTH SEA OIL

The discovery of oil and gas in the North Sea in the 1960s and '70s was to transform the economy of Aberdeen and the North East of Scotland. The largest oil terminal in Europe was completed in 1982 at Sullom Voe in Shetland. Processing the huge Brent and Ninian oil fields, at its operational peak Sullom Voe was handling 1.4 million barrels a day. Aberdeen became the oil capital of Europe, with offices set up there by the world's biggest oil companies and the harbour and airport serving the rigs in the North Sea. North Sea oil made Britain the fifth biggest oil producer in the world and, although the profits did not stay in Scotland, oil has brought long-standing economic prosperity to Aberdeen and Shetland.

Aberdeen also became, briefly, the best football team in Scotland. Under their manager Alex Ferguson (1941–) the team replaced their grey, careful, Granite City image with the more welcoming Furryboots City – which came from the locals' greeting to visitors, 'Far aboots ye fae?' (Whereabouts are you from?).

Other Scots would make cruel comments about Aberdeen's new-found self-confidence and prosperity, but Aberdonians ignored such jealousy as they were too busy finding a secure enough safe in which to deposit their wallet.

THE SNP

1967 saw the SNP's Winnie Ewing (1929–) win a stunning Westminster by-election at Hamilton when she took a formerly safe Labour seat by 1,800 votes. Her victory may have been the result of a short lived protest against the Labour government that had got out of hand, but it shocked the whole of Britain.

Both Labour and Conservative were terrified at the

prospect of a rise in Scottish nationalism and put additional money into the Scottish economy. But the Scottish electorate had become disillusioned with Britain's declining economy and the SNP gained votes from both parties. Unemployment was rising, Scotland's traditional heavy industries were struggling and the British Empire, which had been the great incentive when Scotland signed the Act of Union was no more. Even The Beatles had split up.

The late sixties had also seen the discovery of large oil and gas fields in the North Sea. With Britain facing a series of energy crises culminating in the three-day week of 1973, North Sea Oil had the potential to be Britain's salvation. But the SNP pointed out that as the oil was in the North Sea it belonged to Scotland. They campaigned on the slogan 'It's Scotland's Oil' at the 1974 general election and lots of Scots agreed with them: the SNP returned eleven MPs to Westminster and won thirty per cent of the vote in Scotland.

DEVOLUTION

There were two general elections in 1974 and eventually the Labour Party were returned with a majority of only three. Reluctantly, in response to the SNP's demands for Scottish home rule, Labour agreed to support devolving a degree of autonomy to a new Assembly in Edinburgh. By 1977 Labour had lost their majority in parliament and required support from the SNP among others to continue to govern. A Scotland Bill that proposed Scottish devolution was finally put forward and passed in 1978, but would require the Scottish electorate to vote for it in a referendum to be held in 1979. The proposed Assembly would have no tax-raising powers and fell well short of what the SNP and supporters of independence were looking for, but it was better than nothing.

Scottish self-confidence was unusually high. The Bay City Rollers pop band had brought tartan to the world as they sang *Shang-A-Lang*, honorary Scot Rod Stewart was top of the charts and in 1977 Scotland had not only defeated the English football team at Wembley, but their fans had celebrated by also taking the goal posts and most of the pitch home with them. Furthermore, Scotland had qualified for the 1978 World Cup finals in Argentina, and not only had England failed to qualify but Scotland believed they had a chance of winning the whole thing. Thirty thousand people turned up in Glasgow to wave off the team and their confident manager Ally MacLeod (1934–2004).

Scotland's World Cup campaign was a disaster. They were knocked out in the first round, one of their players, Willie Johnston, was sent home in disgrace, the English found it almost impossible to stop sniggering and the entire Scottish nation felt humiliated and embarrassed.

By the time the devolution campaign began many Scots had lost interest. The Conservatives – who back in 1968 had been keen to support devolution – were now firmly against changing the status quo. The Labour Party, who were officially in favour of devolution, were now divided between those who were against and those who supported it but did not want to campaign with the SNP. One prominent critic was Labour MP Tam Dalyell (1932–) who asked:

'How can it be right that MPs elected to Westminster from Scottish constituencies have no ability to affect the issues of their constituents which have been devolved to the Scottish Parliament.'

and:

'If power over Scottish affairs is devolved to a Scottish Parliament, how can it be right that MPs representing Scottish constituencies in the Parliament of the United Kingdom will have the power to vote on issues affecting England (including those that don't affect Scotland), but English MPs will not have the power to vote on Scottish issues?'

This became known as the West Lothian question, after Dalyell's constituency, and made a change from the other West Lothian question which was:

'Where is West Lothian exactly?'

To confuse matters even further, Labour had by then amended the rules so that it was not just a case of a majority of Scots voting 'yes' for a Scottish Assembly, but forty per cent of the entire electoral roll (including the dead, the infirm, the mad and the bad) had to vote in favour in order for the result to stand.

The devolution referendum was held at the end of the Winter of Discontent during which Britain had suffered a miserable period of strikes and industrial action under an increasingly unpopular and struggling Labour government. The decision of Labour's 'yes' campaign to feature a picture of Prime Minister James Callaghan on their leaflets was, therefore, perhaps not the most beneficial to the cause.

With the 1979 general election imminent and the

Conservatives well ahead in the polls, Alec Douglas-Home (1903–95) – Conservative prime minister from 1963–64 – made a speech promising Scotland something better than the proposed assembly if they voted 'no' to it. He neglected to mention, however, that he was referring to eleven years of being ruled by Margaret Thatcher (1925–).

On 1 March 1979 the Scottish electorate went to the polls. Thirty-three per cent voted for the assembly, thirty-one per cent voted against and thirty-six per cent were washing their hair. The Labour government confirmed that the forty per cent rule applied – the 'yes' vote would not be accepted. The SNP withdrew their support and the Labour government lost a vote of confidence in parliament. At the subsequent May general election, Labour was defeated by the Conservatives and a disillusioned Scottish public turned against the SNP who lost nine of their eleven Westminster MPs.

The original Royal High School building in Edinburgh, which was to be the home of the Scottish Assembly, would remain unoccupied. Ally MacLeod had resigned as Scotland manager, Les McKeown had left the Bay City Rollers and the price of a pint of beer had increased to sixty pence. Sad days indeed.

Now That's What I Call A Post-Industrial Modern Country With Self-Confidence Issues Volume 42

MARGARET THATCHER

When Margaret Thatcher was elected prime minister in 1979, the Conservatives had twenty-two MPs in Scotland, well behind Labour's forty-four, but comfortably in second place. Thatcher's style of Conservative government was radically different from previous administrations. Thatcher believed in the power of the market rather than the state and the rights of the individual rather than the community. Nationalised industries and utilities would be privatised and sold off, traditional industries such as mining and shipbuilding would no longer benefit from government subsidy and the power of the trade unions would be curbed. Local government budgets would be capped and council tenants were given the right to buy their houses.

The car plant at Linwood and the steelworks at Ravenscraig were closed. Shipyards on the Clyde were now reduced to turning out the occasional speedboat. Coal miners, historically at the forefront of the union movement, numbered only 20,000 by 1980. In the bitter strike of 1984 the miners took on the government and lost and by the end of the decade only one Scottish deep-mine colliery was still open. According to government figures, by 1985 unemployment in Scotland had risen to 340,000 – one in seven of the adult population –and a generation of Scots who had depended on employment supported by the state now depended on welfare supported by the state.

Margaret Thatcher was a staunch unionist and all talk of Scottish devolution was ruled out with power in Scotland to remain with the Secretary of State for Scotland – George Younger (1979–86) and Malcolm Rifkind (1986–90) – who would do as he was told or face the full swing of the prime ministerial handbag.

Thatcherism and Scotland did not really get along. If Thatcher said the world was round, then most Scots would reply that the pope spent time in the woods. If the Scots asked for more power or money, the Conservatives would ignore them – which was quite ungrateful really, when you consider that during the eighties the entire British economy was being bankrolled by North Sea oil.

In 1987, the Conservatives won their third consecutive general election, but lost 12 seats in Scotland to leave them with only 10 out of 72. In Scotland, Labour was the dominant party by far, but the Liberals and the SNP were also beginning to gain seats.

Even Mrs Thatcher realised that there may be an issue and decided to spend more time in Scotland. Unfortunately this resulted in the Sermon on the Mound in 1988 when she lectured the Church of Scotland General Assembly – at its headquarters above the Mound in Edinburgh – about Christian values and how St Paul believed in a free market economy. Thatcher followed this up with a visit to Glasgow to attend the Scottish Cup final. Here, not only did she have to present the trophy to a victorious Celtic captain surrounded by a sea of Irish tricolours, but had also been welcomed into the stadium by a 75,000-strong crowd waving red cards and singing, 'Maggie, Maggie, Get To F***'. Diplomatic officials explained to the PM that these were friendly Scots expressing their hope that she would have time to visit the beautiful Kingdom of Fife.

POLL TAX

It was hard to imagine the relationship between Mrs Thatcher and Scotland becoming any worse, but in 1989 the Community Charge or, as it was more popularly known, the Poll Tax was introduced. The poll tax was a new system of raising money to pay for local government. It was bad enough that there was inherent unfairness in that everyone had to pay exactly the same amount no matter how much or how little they earned, but what took the Scottish Digestive, was that the poll tax was to be introduced in Scotland a full year before the rest of Britain – just for sheer devilment.

Many Scots refused to pay the community charge and when opposition intensified in 1990 when it was introduced in England, Margaret Thatcher was finally forced to resign on 28 November, two days before St Andrew's Day. There were calls for a huge Scottish national street party to celebrate, but the weather was a bit nippy, so it was decided not to bother.

RETURN OF THE STONE

The new prime minister was John Major who had the great advantages of not being his predecessor and being able to abolish the community charge/Poll Tax in 1993 and replace it with the council tax. However, he was still a Conservative, and a staunch unionist who rejected all calls for devolution. Nevertheless, in 1996 – one year after the film *Braveheart* had been released – the Conservative government decided to send the Stone of Destiny back to Scotland with a guard of honour. Thus, Scotland was not allowed to make any decisions on education, health or any other issue directly affecting Scotland, but it could just about be trusted to look after some old rock.

The Stone of Destiny is on public display, alongside the Honours of Scotland, in Edinburgh Castle. The stone sits in a glass case but if you look very carefully you can just about see the words LIZ X PI IIL carved on its side.

'GLASGOW'S MILES BETTER'

Scotland's largest city had suffered since World War II. Glasgow was living with industrial decline on the Clyde, rising unemployment, organised crime and the 'razor gangs'. In addition, the city's tenement slums – long overdue for improvement – were being replaced with concrete, high-rise developments; uniform, tower blocks where what you gained in windows and views, you lost in community amenities and living at ground level. Residents would often be asked if they had vertigo to which they would invariably reply, 'no, just round the corner'.

A concerted effort was made by Glasgow in the eighties to renew, regenerate and rebrand. The Burrell Collection was opened in Pollok Country Park in 1983 and became Scotland's most popular visitor attraction at the time.

In the same year, Glasgow Council launched a highly successful campaign based around the slogan 'Glasgow's Miles Better', which did much to transform the stereotype of a city that had been too long associated solely with football, alcoholism and violence – and where a Glasgow kiss was likely to lead to hospital treatment rather than a romantic evening. It was never actually explained whether Glasgow was miles better than it used to be or miles better than somewhere else (Airdrie perhaps), but in the eighties many young people were more than happy to visit a city that had a big yellow smiley face (Mr Happy) as its civic symbol.

Glasgow became European City of Culture in 1990 and will host the 2014 Commonwealth Games

COMEDY

Through the success of Scottish comedians and comic actors on stage and screen, the late 20th century also saw a change in the traditional view of the dour Scot. Alastair Sim (1900–76) from Edinburgh was a popular British film actor, perhaps best known for his dual roles as Miss Fritton, the very tall headmistress and 'her' brother in the St Trinian's films. This previously unacknowledged penchant for Scottish men dressing as women was reinforced by Stanley Baxter (1926–) in his spectacular sixties and early seventies BBC TV series *The Stanley Baxter Show* and in his impression of the queen.

Ronnie Corbett (1930–) from Edinburgh was the smaller of TV's *The Two Ronnies* in the show which ran on BBC 1 from 1971–87. Corbett had a regular slot halfway through the show when he would sit on an armchair and tell a funny story; his jokes were, allegedly, hilarious, but as that was when viewers went off to make a cup of tea nobody ever heard them.

Billy Connolly (1942–) from Glasgow, a former shipyard welder found great success in the seventies playing comedy gigs and shows, making records and appearing on television. Connolly went on to find further fame and respect as an actor playing serious roles, and he gave jokes about jobbies to the world.

TELEVISION

One of the most famous Scots on TV was Montgomery Scott who first appeared as chief engineer on the Starship Enterprise in 1966. 'Scotty' was born in Linlithgow and upheld the long tradition of hard-working but somewhat pessimistic Scottish engineers as he was always to be found in the engine room advising that 'the ship just cannae take it Captain'.

The long-running British sci-fi series *Doctor Who* has had two Scots play the Time Lord. Sylvester McCoy was seventh to play the Doctor with the current incumbent (the tenth) David Tennant (1971–) from Bathgate in the role since 2005.

However, the best-known Scot on TV is Groundskeeper Willie (1991–) from *The Simpsons*. Willie has red hair and a red beard, a fierce demeanour, an incomprehensible accent and unpleasant, villainous tendencies. In other words, the ideal ambassador for 21st-century Scotland

MUSIC

For the first forty years of the 20th century, Scotland's main contribution to international music had been Harry Lauder (1870–1950) from Portobello near Edinburgh, a popular performer around the world who sang and wrote *Keep Right on to the End of the Road* and *Roamin' in the Gloamin'*. In 1964, Lulu from Glasgow was always feeling the urge to Shout on a regular basis and in 1975 the Bay City Rollers from Edinburgh were the biggest band in the UK with *Bye Bye Baby* – they also brought Rollermania and tartan flares to unsuspecting millions.

In the eighties, however, a plethora of singers and groups that included Annie Lennox, Sheena Easton, Simple Minds, Texas, the Proclaimers, Edwyn Collins and the Jesus and Mary Chain established Scotland as a half-decent rock and pop country. But Scotland's most successful musical export are Australian rockers AC/DC, with singer Bon Scott born in Kirriemuir and guitarist brothers Angus and Malcolm Young born in Glasgow. AC/DC recorded the legendary rock albums *Highway to Hell* and *Back In Black* and at one time had their T-shirts worn by half of all white male American teenagers. The band did remain true to their roots when in their classic hit *Whole Lotta Rosie* they declared that the perfect woman had the measurements 42-39-56, so it was presumably somebody Scottish that they were referring to.

NUMBER 1s

The first Scottish singer to get to Number 1 in the UK was Lonnie Donegan (1931–2002) with *Cumberland Gap* in 1957. Donegan would have three Number 1s in total between 1957 and 1960 including *My Old Man's a Dustman* and was known as the King of Skiffle. Although raised in London, Donegan was born in Glasgow, but his father was a violinist and not a dustman.

The first Scottish group to be top of the charts was Marmalade, from Glasgow, and not Dundee as you might expect, and got to Number 1 in 1969 with the Beatles cover *Ob-La-Di Ob-La-Da*.

That song was to usher in a golden era of Scottish music during the seventies with the following Scottish groups reaching the top of the singles charts: *Chirpy Chirpy Cheep Cheep* by Middle Of The Road from Glasgow in 1970; *Amazing Grace* by The Pipes and Drums and Military Band of the Royal Scots Dragoon Guards in 1972, who were known to do gigs at Edinburgh Castle; *January* by Pilot from Edinburgh which curiously got to Number 1 in February; *Bye Bye Baby* and *Give A Little Love* by The Bay City Rollers in 1975; *D.I.V.O.R.C.E* by Billy Connolly in 1975 and *Forever and Ever* by Slik from Glasgow in 1976.

The first Scottish female to get to Number 1 was Lena Martell from Glasgow in 1979 with the gospel song *One Day at a Time.* She was followed by Mary Sandeman who, under her alter-ego Aneka, reached the top of the charts in 1981 with *Japanese Boy,* for which this respected traditional Scottish folk singer dressed up as a geisha.

The Scottish single that held on longest to the UK's Number 1 slot was *Love Is All Around* by Wet Wet Wet from Clydebank. The single reigned for fifteen weeks in 1994, although it seemed much, much longer. In recent years various other Scottish artists have topped the UK singles charts, but luckily Darius, David Sneddon, Michelle McManus and Leon have maintained the quality that Scottish pop music is renowned for.

Special mention should be made of Rod Stewart (1945–) who, although born and bred in London, his father was a Scot and Rod is a keen supporter of the Scottish football team. The singer has had four UK Number 1s to date, the most famous of which was *Maggie May* in 1971 – although if Rod had ever actually lived in Scotland then it would have probably been renamed Maggie May Not.

DOLLY THE SHEEP

Scotland's reputation for scientific innovation was enhanced with the announcement in 1997 that scientists working at the Roslin Institute outside Edinburgh had, during the preceding year, cloned a female sheep – the first mammal to be successfully cloned from an adult somatic cell. The cell had been taken from a mammary gland and the ewe had quite large ears and was given the name Dolly (1996–2003) in appreciation of her big lugs. Dolly's first lamb was named Bonnie. Sadly, Dolly was in some ways a very Scottish sheep as she died from a lung disease at the age of six, well short of her natural life expectancy. Scottish farmers were not impressed by Dolly, prices for sheep were bad enough without someone going around cloning more.

The Return
Of The Jock

TARTAN ARMY

The relationship between England and Scotland had always had a degree of rivalry, resentment and jealousy, but the Thatcher years seemed to turn many Scots into xenophobic racists when it came to their English neighbours. Thankfully, cross-border raiding and laying siege to Berwick had gone out of fashion, so the annual football international became the high point for Anglo-Scottish antipathy. Although by 1989 the atmosphere surrounding these games had become so poisonous that they were abandoned – to the great relief of all concerned.

English football had been scarred by hooliganism and had been banned from European club football. Scottish football realised that they would have to be as different from the English as possible as otherwise they were in danger of also being banned by association. So Scottish supporters who had in the seventies and eighties spent an inordinate amount of time and money on plans to trash London every two years now took a sacred vow to be good-natured, friendly and above all peaceful ambassadors of their country, no matter how much alcohol was consumed. As the world already assumed that Scots routinely wore kilts and 'see you, Jimmy' hats, then that is what they would give them. The Tartan Army was born.

The Tartan Army has become a sporting, social and economic phenomenon. It has travelled from the Faroes to the Ukraine exporting a new brand of Scottishness that consists of eternal cheerfulness in the face of repeated adversity. Scottish supporters were named best fans at the 1992 European championships and the 1998 World Cup finals in France, where 35,000 Scots marched through St Etienne in celebration at finding a pub with Kronenbourg on draught.

In the 21st century, as far as football is concerned it seems Scotland has finally accepted that there is more to life than beating the English; not that this will stop Scots from supporting Portugal, Germany or Trinidad every two years when required.

TARTAN DAY

As well as the Tartan Army, another sign of Scotland's acceptance of its tartan, kilts and bagpipes image is the huge money-spinner that is the Scottish wedding industry. Thousands of pounds are spent on the ideal romantic Scottish wedding: the castle, the lone piper, the ceilidh; men in full dress kilt with all the trimmings and that very traditional Scottish touch – the bow tie. From the kilt's appearance being associated with the Highlands and the upper classes, it is now not uncommon to see herds (or folds) of kilt-wearing wedding guests, champagne glass in hand, contemplating whether or not the bridesmaids will be interested in what they may or may not be wearing underneath said kilt, and carrying appropriate accessories in their sporrans if required.

Even more lucrative than the wedding business is the annual celebration in the US and Canada of Tartan Day and Tartan Week. Officially recognised by the US Senate in 1998 to celebrate the historic links between Scotland and the thirty million Americans who claim Scots descent, Tartan Day is celebrated on 6 April, the anniversary of the Declaration of Arbroath in 1320. As Scotland's attempt to rival the success in the US of St Patrick's Day, Tartan Day has as its main attraction a march of pipers through the streets of New York. So important have the Tartan Day celebrations become to Scotland and Scottish tourism that in 2004 First Minister Jack McConnell wore a pinstripe kilt and white blouse at a Tartan Week fashion show. This resulted in huge criticism for McConnell at home, not because he was belittling the office of First Minister by modelling at a fashion show, but because he didn't wear a sporran.

CEILIDH

Scottish weddings have also sparked a renaissance for Scottish dancing, often referred to as a ceilidh. The word ceilidh is derived from the Gaelic meaning 'visit' and Scottish dancing and music enjoy a long tradition. But despite the support of Queen Victoria and the nobility in the 19th century Scottish dancing was in danger of dying out with the advent of 20th century dance hall music and its ready availability on records from the US. A Scottish dance and music revival began after World War II, inspired by accordionist Jimmy Shand and his band and the TV show *The White Heather Club* (1957–68). The show, in turn, was conclusive proof to the rest of Britain that all Scots wore kilts and were always up for a Highland Fling, as long as they had first had a wee dram.

A Scottish dance band will include accordions and fiddles and will lead dancers in enthusiastic and exuberant jigs, Schottisches and reels such as Strip the Willow, the Dashing White Sergeant, the Eightsome Reel and the Gay Gordons. The Gay Gordons is believed to be named after the Gordon Highlanders, one of Scotland's most famous and respected regiments who were known for their colourful attire and time spent getting ready in the morning. Ceilidhs have today become so popular that some people actually go to more than one a year.

JOHN SMITH

In Britain the Labour Party remained the official opposition to the Conservatives from 1979–97, although the Liberals made progress under their Scottish leader, David Steel (1938–). With Labour support in England at its lowest in fifty years, it was Scottish support for Labour that helped keep them in second place and ensured that Scottish MPs gained senior positions in the party.

The most influential of these Labour MPs was John Smith (1938–94) who was that very rare politician;

somebody who was liked and trusted by the general public. A committed and dedicated supporter of devolution, it was Smith more than anyone who convinced Labour to support what he called, 'the settled will of the Scottish people'. And as Smith was an Advocate as well as a politician, he knew more about wills than most.

John Smith became Labour leader in 1992, but unfortunately after rather than before the general election of the same year. He became a popular leader of the opposition against a very unpopular Conservative government and would, in all probability, have become prime minister – the only question mark being the extent of his majority. Sadly, John Smith died suddenly of a heart attack in 1994. His funeral was in Edinburgh and he was granted the very rare honour of being buried on the holy island of Iona, ancient resting place of more than forty Scottish kings.

TONY BLAIR

When John Smith was Labour leader, it was Shadow Chancellor Gordon Brown (1951–) from Kirkcaldy who was considered heir apparent for the premiership. However, on Smith's death it soon became clear that it was the younger, more photogenic and more English

Tony Blair (1953–) who was favourite to succeed. At a restaurant in London in 1994 the two friends, and now rivals, met to discuss the party's future. Brown agreed that he would stand aside in order to allow Blair to lead a new and reforming Labour into the next general election and beyond. In return Blair agreed that he would get the bill.

Tony Blair was actually born in Edinburgh and was a boarder at Fettes College, an Edinburgh fee-paying school, but he spent most of his childhood in England, where he remained through university, as a pupil barrister and as MP for an English constituency, Sedgefield. Much in the same way that he didn't do God, Blair didn't really do Scotland either. He did however condone Labour's support for devolution in Scotland, which would be a key manifesto promise in the run-up to the 1997 general election.

ALEX SALMOND

After a difficult and disappointing decade in the eighties the SNP elected a new leader, Alex Salmond (1954–), in 1990. Under Salmond and with the party's continued policy of independence for Scotland while remaining within the European Union, the SNP began slowly to progress. In the 1992 general election the SNP won more than twenty per cent of the popular vote for the first time since 1974. Numerous opinion polls were held in the ensuing period up until 1997 to determine the degree of support for independence within Scotland. The results of these polls varied wildly, and were likely influenced by how the Scottish football team had performed or whether the respondents had seen *Braveheart* the night before.

When the SNP's Jim Sillars lost his Govan seat in the 1992 general election he coined the phrase 'ninety-minute patriots' – on the basis that the only time Scots were actively patriotic was when watching a football match. This was, of course, completely unfair; when Scotland is losing badly, most Scots leave the ground long before the ninety minutes is up.

While support both for the SNP and for independence was increasing, as far as Scotland was concerned, it was first things first: which meant getting rid of the Tories.

1997 GENERAL ELECTION

At the 1997 general election, the number of SNP MPs in Westminster increased from three to six, but more significantly the party moved into second place of the popular vote (behind Labour) in Scotland. The

Liberal Democrats won ten seats and would see popular Highland MP Charles Kennedy become party leader in 1999. But on 1 May 1997 Labour won a landslide victory, and in Scotland achieved their best ever result with 56 out of 72 seats and forty-five per cent of the Scottish vote.

A jubilant Tony Blair brought to an end eighteen years of Conservative government with the words, 'a new dawn has broken, has it not?', which most people thought was a tad harsh on new Dawn, whoever she was.

For the Conservatives the election was a disaster. While surprised to have been re-elected in 1992, the 1997 result was worse than any Conservative had feared. In Scotland, most people had seen their standard of living rise, unemployment fall, the economy grow and the housing market boom, but this did nothing to stop Scots voting out all remaining ten Scottish Conservative MPs and wipe them off the political map.

Senior Conservative MPs, such as cabinet ministers Malcolm Rifkind, Ian Lang and Michael Forsyth, were all defeated by the cunning plan of Labour, SNP and Liberal supporters to vote together against them. The party who had won more than fifty per cent of the Scottish vote in 1955 now had zero seats; Scotland had finally gained their revenge on the party of Mrs Thatcher.

DONALD DEWAR

The new Labour government had a considerable influence in Scotland. Blair may not have considered himself Scottish, but there were seven Scots in his first Cabinet including Gordon Brown as Chancellor, Robin Cook as Foreign Secretary and Donald Dewar (1937–2000) as Scottish Secretary. Scots had not experienced so much power at Westminster since the time of James VI, and some English political commentators complained about being governed by a Scottish Raj. Ministers were quick to reject such accusations as utter nonsense and saw nothing wrong with lunch at the weekly cabinet meetings now being a roll and sausage and a bottle of ginger.

Dewar was an experienced and respected figure who had first been Labour's Scottish spokesman back in 1983. He came from Glasgow, had been a close friend and ally of John Smith's, a dedicated supporter of devolution and had been given responsibility – after the Scottish Assembly debacle of 1979 – for making sure that a Scottish parliament would, this time, come into being.

However, before any legislation was introduced,

Prime Minister Blair insisted on a referendum in Scotland to establish support for the creation of a Scottish parliament. Controversially, the referendum would include a second question: should the Scottish parliament have tax-varying powers?

The right to raise finance had been excluded from the 1979 devolution proposals and had been widely accepted as making the Assembly of 1979 no more than a glorified debating chamber. Most people believed that tax-raising was essential for a Scottish parliament and therefore asking a specific separate question on it was an attempt by Blair to water down devolution. Labour denied this was the case and Blair quietly dropped plans for a double or quits third question – Scots would be offered an all-expenses-paid-holiday to Blackpool if Scotland agreed to keep the status quo.

REFERENDUM 1997

The referendum – the second on Scottish devolution – would be held on 11 September 1997. Labour, the SNP and the Liberal Democrats agreed to work together to support a 'yes/yes' vote. The dream team – Blair, Dewar, Salmond and Sean Connery – campaigned, Scottish newspapers, on the whole, backed devolution and there were no Conservative

MPs remaining north of the border to put the opposition's view. Even the death of Diana, Princess of Wales less than two weeks prior to the referendum did not postpone the vote, though sadly we will never know if the People's Princess would have supported Scottish tax-varying powers.

Those who wanted devolution had never had a better opportunity for success, but now it was all down to the Scottish people and nobody knew which way they would vote. As Labour supporter and Aberdeen then Manchester United football manager Alex Ferguson once said, it was 'squeaky bum time'.

Incredibly, and in the most remarkable and unprecedented show of national self-confidence, the Scottish electorate decided overwhelmingly to vote 'yes' to the first Scottish parliament in 290 years, by 74 per cent to 26 per cent. Not only that, but of their own free and against all expectations the canny Scots voted an overwhelming 'yes', by 64 per cent to 36 per cent, to the prospect of being taxed to high heaven. Even the infamous 'forty per cent of the entire electorate' rule from the 1979 Assembly vote had been exceeded.

SCOTTISH ELECTION 1999

Preparations began for the first elections to the new Scottish parliament. There would be a fairly hefty

129 MSPs – 73 constituency MSPs, and 56 list regional MSPs. In return there would be a reduction of Scottish MPs at Westminster.

The devolved Scottish parliament would legislate on matters including health, education, law and order, local government, transport, small business or commerce, agriculture, fishing, housing and the environment, tourism, sport and the arts. Reserved powers, retained by the UK government at Westminster included foreign affairs, defence, taxation, social services and scary things like war, nuclear power, 'mad cow disease' and the *National Lottery* Saturday night TV show. Acts of God it was agreed would be dealt with on an Act by Act basis, depending on how wrathful God had decided to be.

Donald Dewar decided he did not want the new parliament to take over the former Royal High School building, which for twenty years had been proposed to house the administration. Instead, Dewar wanted to commission a new building, designed from scratch. This decision was highly controversial. Some politicians were aghast at the additional cost, some were suspicious that Labour was seeking to hide parliament away rather than create a national icon on Calton Hill.

In January 1998 Dewar chose a site at Holyrood –

opposite Holyrood Palace – on land where there had once been a brewery. Designs for the building were tendered and the one chosen was by innovative Catalan architect Enric Miralles (1955–2000). The hope was that the new parliament would be ready for the first general election of the Scottish parliament in 1999; sadly, this hope was soon scuppered. A government white paper mentioned that the project's total budget would be £40 million, although it neglected to mention that this figure was for the canteen and stationery cupboard only.

In May 1999 elections took place for the new Scottish parliament and for the four main parties the results were relatively encouraging. Labour under Dewar came top with fifty-six MSPs, not enough for an outright majority but comfortably in first place; the SNP under Salmond, who many had predicted would have no role in Scottish politics post-devolution, came second with thirty-five; the Liberal Democrats gained seventeen seats and agreed to join Labour to form the first government and enough Conservatives came out of their witness-protection programme to win eighteen seats.

1999 PARLIAMENT

So, with the Holyrood site nothing more than a huge big hole in the ground, it was in the Assembly Hall of the Church of Scotland that the newly elected MSPs met on 12 May 1999 to reconvene the first Scottish parliament for 270 years. Winnie Ewing, the veteran SNP whose victory at Hamilton back in 1967 began the whole devolution debate, was given the honour of being the first MSP to speak in the new parliament and uttered the immortal words, 'Is it on?' in reference to whether or not the microphones were working.

Donald Dewar was appointed First Minister (Scotland's prime minister), former Liberal leader David Steel was appointed Presiding Officer (Scotland's Speaker) and the Government was to be known as the Scottish Executive, rather than the Scottish government, and would be supplied with a free newspaper, freshly made coffee and extra leg room.

Of the 129 newly elected MSPs only fourteen were currently MPs at Westminster. Most of Scotland's Westminster politicians preferred to stay within the institution and expenses that they new best rather than transfer to the untried and untested Scottish Executive. Concerns were raised about the quality and the experience of the MSPs and the Presiding Officer had to explain that it was not necessary to put your hand up if you wished to go to the bathroom. But the general mood was one of hope and optimism and the

Scottish parliament was in celebratory mood. On the night of 12 May the MSPs decided to party like it was 1999 – which, conveniently, it was.

The Future Is Bright
And Probably Not
Brown

IMMIGRATION

Asians began emigrating from the Subcontinent to
Scotland from the 1950s. The 2001 census shows the
Asian population in Scotland standing at around
50,000 or one per cent of the total Scottish
population. The Asian influence on Scotland,
however, along with the smaller Chinese and
Italian-Scottish communities, far exceeds their small
numbers. The nation's culinary habits have been
transformed with generations of Scots experiencing
international cuisine through such innovations of

pizza, crispy duck, chips and curry sauce, or the even more exotic chips, cheese and curry sauce.

There has been a Polish community in Scotland since World War II when members of the exiled Polish Armed Forces were based in England and Scotland and fought in the British army. Since Poland joined the European Union in 2004, some 60,000 to 100,000 Poles have come to live in Scotland, much to the relief of Scottish employers who were previously struggling to recruit locals who could speak good English.

Even with the increasing number of Eastern Europeans, the biggest number of non-Scots living in Scotland is by far and away the English, with 2001 estimates at 350,000 and rising. Although there has been friction, especially in the Highlands where the English are not infrequently referred to as White Settlers, relations on the whole are harmonious, with any resentment towards English neighbours dwindling to nothing when compensated by the amusement factor of hearing a Southerner say the words 'Oor Wullie'.

Scotland is becoming more multi-cultural, while the increase in the number of English and Polish immigrants has reinforced the fact that ninety-eight per cent of people living in Scotland were white – or to give the correct anthropological definition white with a slight touch of ginger.

The last census of most common Scottish surnames in 2001 showed that the most popular surnames had altered little over the past century. In order of frequency they were Smith, Brown, Wilson, Stewart, Thomson, Campbell, Robertson, Anderson, Scott and MacDonald. Interestingly, they were only four other Mac (Mc) surnames in the top fifty (MacKenzie, MacKay, MacLeod and MacLean) and according to the census all the Thatchers in Scotland had unsurprisingly left the country.

HOLYROOD

Expectations were very high for the new Scottish Executive and parliament, with the public demanding nothing less than that all aspects of Scottish life should be immediately transformed for the better, and for Scotch eggs to be free at all outlets. Sadly, the executive failed to meet these expectations and the public and the media began to criticise. MSPs were nicknamed 'numpties' and said to be unable to organise a piss-up either in a brewery or – as far as the Holyrood parliament project was concerned – on a former brewery site.

Holyrood was by 2000 seriously over budget and behind schedule and would suffer twin blows by the deaths within four months of each other of both the architect Enric Miralles and First Minister Donald Dewar. As had been the case when his friend and Labour colleague John Smith died, Donald Dewar's sudden death engendered great sadness throughout the country; it also robbed the parliament of its most experienced and respected member.

On 9 October 2004, Presiding Officer George Reid asked the Queen to open the Holyrood parliament building. It was five years late and, at a total of £430 million, had cost more than ten times the original estimate. The sun, however, was shining and for all concerned there was relief that the building was finally finished. Architecturally, Holyrood had strong and mixed reactions: some thought it ugly and ill-suited to the landscape, with more than a passing similarity to a 1970s local council building; others praised Holyrood as one of the most exciting and innovative public buildings in Europe, deserving of all the awards it won in the UK and Spain, and cheap at the price.

The Holyrood building became a popular tourist attraction, with thousands of Scots and foreign visitors curious to see what all the controversy was about – and what all that money had gone towards. The majority came to the conclusion that the building was all right, but they could do with cutting the grass more often.

BLAIR AND BROWN

Tony Blair had comfortably won two further general elections in 2001 and 2005 to become the most successful and longest serving Labour prime minister in British history – although many members and supporters were never actually sure what Blair and the Labour Party had in common. The Blair government had undertaken radical constitutional reform and, under the iron chancellor Gordon Brown, had worked towards establishing a stable economy. Blair had proved a popular leader, although noticeably less so in Scotland where there remained innate suspicion of politicians with a permanent grin on their face.

The Blair/Brown partnership had been the cornerstone of New Labour's government, although since Brown stood aside for Blair back in 1994 their relationship had become increasingly strained. Which of the two men was in charge? Blair was Labour Party leader and prime minister, Brown ran the economy. Blair enjoyed all the kudos and the glory that came with being a statesman, while Brown gloomily pondered post-neoclassical endogenous growth theory while he waited in Number 11 for his time to come.

Blair's popularity would be seriously undermined by his decision in 2003 to join with the US in invading Iraq in order to topple the regime of Saddam Hussein.

Despite huge opposition, Blair had staked his entire reputation on the premiss that the invasion was justified because Iraq possessed weapons of mass destruction and was, therefore, an imminent threat to Britain. Unfortunately, this did not turn out to be the case, although on the bright side, the fact that Iraq did not actually possess weapons of mass destruction made the invasion a lot easier. Initially the invasion seemed to go well with Saddam swifty defeated, but it soon became clear that nobody had any idea about what to do next.

There was much speculation about whether Blair would stand aside for Brown in advance of the 2005 general election. Eventually, the prime minister decided to stay on and go for a third term, but with the proviso that he would not go for a fourth. Speculation now turned to what would happen next . . . Would Blair be brave enough to sack Brown? Or would Brown finally snap and lamp Blair in the middle of a cabinet meeting?

The Election in 2005 saw their relationship shift; to secure victory Blair required Brown to campaign alongside him and, immediately Blair's victory was secured, speculation grew about when Blair would stand down. With the war in Iraq going from bad to worse to truly dreadful, Blair finally agreed, in 2006, that he would stand down in 2007 – but not until he had completed ten years as prime minister, and not until he could find someone, anyone, to take on Brown for the party leadership and the premiership. Sadly for Blair, the only candidate he could find was his Home Secretary and former bare-knuckle boxer John Reid, but Reid was also Scottish and considered somewhat of a risk in polite society.

2007 SCOTTISH ELECTION

By the third Scottish elections in May 2007, people had become more accustomed to the Scottish parliament. The furore surrounding the Holyrood building may neither have been forgiven nor forgotten, but it was no longer the huge issue it had been up until 2004. By 2007 most Scots had become used to the fact that it was the parliament who dealt with and decided on most of the everyday issues that affected their lives, even if they had no idea who their MSP was.

Since 2001 First Minister Jack McConnell (1960–) had led a Labour-Liberal coalition. McConnell's administration had grown enough in confidence to implement radical legislation such as the ban on smoking in 2006 long before anybody else in Britain, but had been tainted by the UK Labour Party's continued support for the war in Iraq. First Minister McConnell's unfortunate mission statement on taking office decreed that his goal would be to 'do less, better' which most people took to mean doing as little as humanly possible at all given times.

But Scotland's ban on smoking in enclosed public spaces precipitated a major change in the way Scots socialised. The centuries-old tradition of a pint and a fag at the pub came to an abrupt end and the most unlikely of establishments adopted tables outside – Continental style – even when temperatures headed towards freezing.

Scotland also became first in the UK to see the phenomenon of 'smirting' (drunken smoking and flirting), a combination which if John Knox had still been alive would have made him so angry that his beard would probably have spontaneously combusted.

Alex Salmond had successfully led the SNP through the nineties, but stood down in 2000. However, in 2004 he returned as leader with the goal of winning the 2007 Scottish elections. Salmond was a clever and populist politician whose cheeky and sometimes abrasive persona had in the past both attracted and alienated voters. The new Salmond was determined to soften his image and become more statesmanlike – he, therefore, had to refrain from laughing at Jack McConnell in public. This policy seemed to be proving effective, as by the beginning of 2007 the SNP were actually ahead in the opinion polls.

The Labour election campaign was somewhat disastrous. The Iraq war remained hugely unpopular, with Scottish soldiers in Basra now among the thousands who had died there since 2003. Prime Minister Tony Blair had yet to stand down despite being warned that in Scotland he was an electoral liability.

In Scotland, First Minister McConnell initially seemed to take the viewpoint that the public did not like seeing politicians on TV and declined all interviews – a perfectly reasonable point of view, but perhaps not the best strategy two months before an election. Divisions also appeared between the Scottish and UK Labour parties about who was actually running the campaign and what their strategy was. The Scottish Labour Party were keen to promote their record in government over the past eight years, their achievements and their exciting programme for the future, to which UK Labour said, 'bugger that' and decided on a wholly negative campaign equating the SNP to al-Qaeda, the Four Horsemen of the Apocalypse and Scrappy Doo.

3 MAY 2007

Scotland went to the polls on 3 May 2007 inspired by the final clarion calls of the two biggest Scottish tabloids, the *Scottish Sun* and the *Daily Record*, to vote Labour. The *Scottish Sun* in particular had a charming front page featuring an SNP logo in the shape of a hangman's noose and captioned, 'Vote SNP today and you put Scotland's head in the noose'. At least the *Sun* abandoned plans for their free noose election giveaway.

All the opinion polls predicted an election that would be too close to call – anything could happen, they said. They did not predict however that the new electronic vote-counters would break down and that a change in the ballot paper design would result in 140,000 voters, predominantly in West and Central Scotland, getting their knots and crosses mixed up and inadvertently spoiling their paper. In the good old days there used to be just one big box and an arrow pointing to one big sign that read 'Vote Labour'.

Scotland woke up on the morning of 4 May 2007 to discover that nobody knew who had won and that most of the vote-counting still had to be done. It was not until five o' clock that evening that the very last votes were counted – in the Highlands & Islands Region. The final result had been about to be announced – a Labour victory – when the SNP candidate for Highlands & Islands, David Thompson, realised that no one had counted his votes. After a frantic search to find somebody in the building who could do long division, Thompson was elected as the forty-seventh SNP MSP – which was one MSP more than Labour's forty-six. Incredibly, Labour had lost their first election in Scotland for more than fifty years. The SNP had topped the poll for the very first time. And as all concerned had not slept for more than thirty-five hours, everyone went to bed.

SALMOND, BROWN AND FERGUSON

Alex Salmond became Scotland's First Minister on 16 May 2007. One of his earliest decisions was to change the name of the Scottish Executive to the Scottish Government. There was no agreement with the Liberal Democrats to form a coalition, so the SNP administration would be run as a minority, with every proposal having to find support from at least one of the Unionist parties.

The Labour Party dealt with their defeat by pretending it was all a bad dream and that one morning they would step out of the shower and everything would be back to normal. For everybody else, an SNP government did not appear to result in the end of the world; Scotland was not assailed by war, famine, death or pestilence, although a nasty flu bug did do the rounds. After waiting seventeen years since first becoming SNP leader, First Minister Salmond had cause to feel a little smug, although he tried not to show it.

Gordon Brown finally became prime minister on 27 June 2007 after Tony Blair – having handcuffed himself to the Cabinet table – had been physically removed from Downing Street. In his first prime ministerial address Brown evoked his Kirkcaldy High School motto, 'I will try my utmost', although missed out the second half, 'not to run in the corridor'.

Many had predicted that Scottish devolution would make it almost impossible for a Scot to become prime minister as the English would not accept being led by someone whose decisions would not necessarily affect his own constituents. Few, however, had foreseen Scotland being run by a party other than Labour. But, as it turned out, with Brown appointing Edinburgh MP Alistair Darling as his chancellor, Govan-born Alex Ferguson winning a record ninth English premiership as manager of Manchester United and Kirsty Young taking over as host of Radio 4's *Desert Island Discs*, as far as the English were concerned having Scots in charge just seemed to be the natural way of things.

BROWN AND SALMOND

The West Lothian question still remained, but was temporarily ignored. The prime minister was making great play about Britain and Britishness, forgetting that as with *Fight Club*, the very first rule of being British is that you don't talk about it.

The first few months of the Brown Premiership went far better than expected as the British public quickly forgot about the previous prime minister – whatever his name was. Brown was encouraged to call a quick general election in October 2007 to secure a personal mandate, but despite favourable opinion polls his innate caution saw him decline to do so. After all, he had waited well over a decade to become prime minister and the thought of rejection after only four months would be just too much to bear.

The cancellation of the election that never was saw an abrupt end to Gordon Brown's honeymoon period. An economic downturn, banks going bankrupt, funding scandals in the Labour Party and poor opinion polls bedevilled his premiership. Tough times lay ahead for Brown and Darling, his faithful chancellor in their quest to secure a historic, fourth successive

Labour victory. Perhaps it is too soon to write off the clunking but increasingly rusty fist of Irn Broon, but it became increasingly clear that Brown was unpopular as prime minister, not because he is Scottish but because he was not very good at it. Rather than becoming the new John Smith he had turned into the new John Major.

While Brown suffered setbacks, the SNP government of the new Republic of Salmondia continued to grow in confidence. The Party was buoyant, finding public support for their populist policies, having their first budget successfully passed by parliament and seeing Glasgow chosen to host the 2014 Commonwealth Games. Trouble, in the form of their proposed abolition of the council tax and increasing disputes between Westminster and the Scottish Government, no doubt lies ahead for the SNP – a minority of eighteen in Holyrood is, after all, not ideal. But one year after their historic election victory there seemed to be little sign of the grin being wiped off wee Alex's face anytime soon.

The Labour opposition in Holyrood led by Wendy Alexander remained in disarray, edging towards new policies and asking for more powers for Parliament – but always having first to ask Gordon's permission. In a bizarre attempt to stop the SNP's momentum,

Alexander announced in May 2008 that unionist Labour, after decades of opposition, would now support a referendum on Scottish independence. The SNP, who until that point would not have been able to get a majority in parliament for a referendum could not believe their luck and announced that, in return, they would support Wendy's leadership of the Labour Party until independence was safely achieved. Unfortunately for Nationalist supporters everywhere, Wendy resigned two months later.

BANKING (PART TWO)

When in June 2008, the good people of the East End of Glasgow sensationally elected SNP candidate John Mason as their Westminster MP in what had been for 60 years one of the safest Labour seats in the country, it all seemed to be over for Prime Minister Brown. The date of the by-election had also been carefully chosen by Labour to be in the middle of the summer holidays so as to reduce the possibility of a large protest vote, not realising that in this time of the credit crunch a lot of people had decided that they could not afford to go to Magaluf and blamed Labour accordingly.

However, when the credit crunch soon escalated into a credit slump and banks around the world began crashing with billions and trillions of debt, it was Brown and Chancellor Darling who sprang into action, re-capitalising the banks, borrowing billions and criss-crossing the globe to organise a co-ordinated international strategy to combat the economic crisis. For the first time in a year, Prime Minister Brown seemed a man at ease, almost happy, in his job and the polls began to respond in his favour.

It was the two big Scottish banks, the Royal Bank of Scotland and Halifax Bank of Scotland, who were the hardest hit in the financial maelstrom of 2008. It became clear that both of these institutions had possible debts larger than the entire budget of Scotland and the markets responded by driving the share price down to the floor.

For First Minister Salmond and the SNP government there was little they could do as power and decision-making over the economy remained in London. Salmond's often repeated claim that Scotland could join Iceland, Ireland and Norway in the 'Arc of Prosperity' came back to haunt him as Iceland's entire economy went bankrupt, even though the first minister explained that it had actually been the frozen food retail chain with the very reasonably priced party food that he had been referring to.

In late 2008 there was a brief moment when it felt

that normal service would be resumed. The banking crisis had been averted, the economy had been stabilised and Labour could dream of winning both the next Westminster and Holyrood elections, although when Brown announced in the House of Commons that he had 'saved the world' it was genuinely thought that our heroic prime minister was being ever so slightly optimistic.

True enough, by the beginning of 2009 it was clear that Supergordon's powers were on the wane. Recession had kicked in, the retail sector was in freefall, unemployment was on the rise, the pound was in steep decline, the banks required even further billions to stay afloat and the public remembered who had been in charge of the economy for the past 12 years.

In Scotland, HBOS, rather than go bankrupt, was taken over by Lloyds, and doubts remain whether their headquarters on the Mound, which have dominated the Edinburgh skyline and the Scottish financial sector since 1806, will be much more than the museum that was opened there in 2006. And the mighty Royal Bank of Scotland, financial masters of the universe just a few months before, also announced in January 2009 the biggest loss in UK history of £28 billion, resulting in a share price that had stood at £5.60 at the end of 2007 crashing to just 11p, and the UK government being forced to take a majority stake in the bank. No one was certain about what the future would hold, other than the carefully cultivated reputation of Scottish banking – one of thrift, caution, hard work and common sense that had been built up over centuries, recognised and appreciated throughout the world – being destroyed in just under six months. Scary times indeed, or as Humphrey Bogart almost said in Casablanca 'it doesn't take much to see that in this crazy mixed-up world the entire worth of the Scottish banking system don't even amount to a tin of beans'.

Auld Lang Fine or Auld Lang Whine

There is a famous saying that history is always repeating itself which is of course not true, as if that were the case then, for example, the Vikings would still be raping and pillaging, there would still be a Stewart king of Scotland and the Scottish football team would always be suffering a last-minute, valiant but glorious defeat – well, maybe history does repeat itself sometimes.

What is more accurate is that history has a habit of seeing events or eras that have similarities with other events and eras, or as Eric Morecambe once said when playing Grieg's Piano Concerto, he was playing the right notes but not necessarily in the right order. Times of decline are followed by times of prosperity, war is followed by peace, successful monarchs are followed by not so successful monarchs, political power is transferred from one party to another and the invention of the wheel is but a forerunner for the invention of stabilisers. Why, even the TV series *Taggart*, that perennial international symbol of the best of the West of Scotland, continues to solve crimes, despite Taggart having died in 1994.

Of course the ever-changing process that is history is one that, while it fascinates historians, can be a complete bugger when trying to write a conclusion to an up-to-date book on the subject of Scottish history. While it is unlikely that we will see in the next few months the return of the Jacobites or discover what really is buried underneath Rosslyn Chapel – other than some old Irn-Bru bottles that the builders left behind – as far as contemporary Scottish politics is concerned we are living in exciting and unpredictable times.

As recently as 1997 decisions in Scotland were made by the Conservative secretary of state Michael Forsyth. Now, in 2009 we have an SNP government, in a Holyrood parliament, proposing a referendum on Scottish independence. It is also likely that by 2010

Labour will be defeated at Westminster by a Conservative Party run by Old Etonians with no more than three or four MPs in Scotland voted in by an English electorate fed up being run by grumpy Scots and if the rest of the Jocks want independence then they are welcome to it. A set of circumstances that only a few years ago the most optimistic of Scottish Nationalists could not have dreamed of, even after a Lagavulin or three.

Whichever party or parties win power at Holyrood and Westminster in the future it seems increasingly likely that, sooner rather than later, the great Scottish public are going to be asked whether, after 300 years of being part of the United Kingdom they wish to be an independent nation again and have their own entry in the Eurovision Song Contest, with Darius already keen to take part.

Whether the historically conservative, contrary and chronically lacking in self-confidence Scots are likely to vote 'yes' remains to be seen. Recent polls indicate that although support for the SNP is rising, support for independence remains well short of a majority. It has even been argued that it is not in the SNP's interest to call for a referendum on independence that they are likely to lose. But even if they do lose then, not to worry, they will of course just keep calling referenda until the exhausted electorate cannot take it any longer and finally vote, 'All right then, noo gi'e us peace'.

The most remarkable thing about Scottish history is that the whole question of Scotland as a nation is still relevant today. If nearly 2,000 years ago the Romans had not decided that Caledonia was a midge-infested land of illiterate barbarians worth nothing more than a couple of big walls, then the island of Britain would have been politically united from the 1st century AD. Again, in the 9th and the 10th centuries, it is perfectly conceivable that if the Vikings had put their minds to it they could have conquered the four kingdoms that then made up Scotland. The Vikings decided instead to concentrate on the richer pickings of England and Normandy, using the Northern and Western Isles only as convenient stop-overs to break the long journey and stock up on duty free.

The very creation of Scotland was also to take centuries: Kenneth MacAlpin united the Scots and Picts in 843, Lothian joined in 1018 and Strathclyde in 1034; the Western Isles were won back from Norway in 1266 but Orkney and Shetland were not part of Scotland until 1472. Throughout much of this time Scotland was riven by incessant civil wars while its various regions were ruled by independent warlords, nobles and chieftains – the power of the king sometimes reaching no further than whichever castle he was staying in at the time and in the case of the several monarchs who were murdered, sometimes not even that far. Furthermore, the country was not even that Scottish: the Scots came from Ireland and the Vikings from Scandinavia; the Angles came from England and the Normans came originally from France; the poor old locals – the Picts – disappeared, leaving their big slabs of squiggly carved stone behind.

And, of course, there were the English. As soon as England became a unified state in the 10th century, its rulers considered it their right to subjugate Scotland and that, at some point, they would get around to doing so. Thankfully for the Scots, the English – like the Vikings and the Romans before them – usually had other things on their minds – usually the French – and give or take numerous wars and battles, England left Scotland to her own devices.

On the two occasions, 1286–90 and 1542–67, when Scotland found itself with a queen as monarch, a union of the crowns was proposed so that England could gain Scotland without too much bother. Neither of these proposed unions happened: in 1290 the young Queen Margaret (Maid of Norway) died in

Orkney and, in 1548, Mary, Queen of Scots was sent to France to marry the heir to the French throne.

So, despite constantly losing battles and having every second monarch crowned while still at play school, the proud nation state of Scotland continued, if not to thrive exactly, then at least in the new Presbyterianism of the Reformation, to endure.

Even after the Act of Union in 1707, when Scotland finally gave up its parliament and became proud North Britons of the burgeoning British Empire, the Scottish nationality survived. Scottish people travelled around the world in their thousands. Innovative Scots changed the world forever with inventions including the steam engine, the telephone, the bicycle, television and penicillin. Writers such as Robert Burns, Sir Walter Scott and Robert Louis Stevenson, and philosophers including David Hume and Adam Smith – all were Scots of international renown. Throughout the world, Scotland's voice has ever been heard – even though with Mike Myers voicing *Shrek* you sometimes wished otherwise.

Scotland has even survived determined attempts by everyone from Queen Victoria to the Scottish Tourist Board to turn the country into their picture postcard image: tartan, Jacobites, whisky, shortbread and small annoying dogs. Striking images promote the picturesque lochs, mountains and glens of the Highlands, but no one mentions that the reason there are no people in the photographs is because everybody has left.

If the world wants to see a monster in a loch, then the Scots will provide some painted tyres; if the world thinks the Scots drink a lot, then the Scots will drink even more and if the world wants to know what is under a Scotsman's kilt, then let the fit ones look.

Perhaps, after all, we should remember the words and sentiments of the most important document in Scottish history, the Declaration of Arbroath. Signed in 1320, six years after the Battle of Bannockburn, the Declaration of Arbroath sets out the case for the right of the Scottish people to be an independent sovereign state in language that is universal and relevant to every nation in the world, as long as you can read Latin, and includes words that have never been surpassed in defining the history of Scotland:

'For so long as but a hundred remain alive, there will always be an *Oor Wullie* annual (except in the years that it is *The Broons* instead).'

TIMELINE

84   Roman army defeats Caledonian tribes at the battle of Mons Graupius. First Scottish pizzeria opens not long after.

563   Saint Columba leaves Ireland with twelve companions and establishes monastery on the island of Iona. Tensions run high about who gets picked at the weekly five-a-side football match.

795   First of many Viking raids on Iona takes place. Home insurance premiums on the island go through the roof.

954   Scots capture Edinburgh from the Northumbrians. Excited local residents celebrate by 'having their tea' thirty minutes later than usual.

1263   Alexander III defeats the Norwegians at the Battle of Largs, so ending Norse rule in the Hebrides. Pickled herring sales go into decline.

1292   John Balliol crowned king of Scotland after being chosen ahead of the other twelve claimants to the vacant throne. The judges are especially impressed by John's Viennese waltz although his rumba could be improved.

1296   Edward I of England, Hammer of the Scots, invades and conquers Scotland. He establishes Hammer Time and removes the Stone of Destiny to England where it is guarded with a large sign stating, as far as Scots are concerned, 'U Can't Touch This'.

1305   William Wallace is hanged, drawn, decapitated and quartered in London. Sadly he does not survive.

1314   Robert the Bruce leads the Scots to victory over the English at the Battle of Bannockburn. English king Edward II returns to London where he is reported to be thinking again.

1346   David II captured by the English and held prisoner for eleven years. He is allowed to keep his crown but can only wear it for thirty minutes a day.

1413   Scotland's first university is founded at St Andrews. To encourage numbers, students are offered a free pack of golf balls.

1437   James I dies in Perth. His body is found to have been stabbed twenty-eight times. Foul play is suspected.

1513   James IV is defeated and killed at the Battle of Flodden. Not a good day.

1542   James V dies and is succeeded by his six-day-old daughter Mary. Especially small crown made for the occasion.

1559   Protestant preacher John Knox dramatically returns to Scotland after a 13-year exile. His faithful colleague Shep stays in quarantine.

1560 Act of Reformation is passed and Scotland officially becomes a Protestant nation. A disappointed Pope cancels his caravan holiday to Skye.

1567 Mary, Queen of Scots is forced to abdicate in favour of her twelve-month-old son James VI. Yet another small crown has to be made.

1603 James VI of Scotland becomes James I of England. He suffers considerable neck pain on his coronation day as a result of having to wear both crowns simultaneously.

1638 National Covenant signed at Greyfriars in Edinburgh. Greyfriars Bobby refuses to sign.

1649 Charles I beheaded in London. He also suffers considerable neck pain.

1650 Oliver Cromwell and his army invade Scotland. They are greeted by many inquisitive Scots, curious to see how round their heads really are.

1660 Charles II restored as king of both England and Scotland. He decides not to bother with the Scottish crown.

1695 Bank of Scotland established. Scotsmen everywhere ponder what they should now put under their beds.

1707 Act of Union between parliaments of England

and Scotland. After extensive negotiations it is agreed that the Scottish parliament will cease to exist and that the Westminster canteen will start serving roll and sausage in the mornings.

1746 Final Jacobite rising ends at the Battle of Culloden. Jacobites disappear from history before reappearing as mini cream crackers.

1748 Acclaimed academic David Hume charged with heresy by the Church of Scotland. On hearing the news Hume, 37, was said to be philosophical.

1842 First Glasgow to Edinburgh train service starts, so beginning one of the great mysteries of Scottish life: where is Polmont? And why are we stopping there?

1876 Scots-born inventor Alexander Graham Bell makes the first phone call. The call takes place at 6pm on a Sunday to take advantage of cheap rates.

1890 Forth Bridge is completed. Good news for local painters.

1906 Keir Hardie founds British Labour Party. According to historical records it was a Socialist party.

1914 World War I begins. Nobody gets home for Christmas.

1934 Scottish National Party is founded. Nobody
notices for thirty-two years.

1942 Mystery surrounds the arrival in Scotland of
Deputy Führer Rudolf Hess. Why of all the places
in the world did he decide to fly to Lanarkshire?

1945 World War II ends. Thank God for that.

1967 Queen Elizabeth II launched at the Clyde.
Diving teams successfully rescue Her Majesty
from the river.

1999 Scottish parliament reconvenes for the first time
since 1707. Menzies Campbell declines to take
up his old seat.